WALKING - - - - - ->
DENVER

32 Tours of the Mile High City's Best Urban Trails, Historic Architecture, and Cultural Highlights

Second Edition

Mindy Sink
with Sophie Seymour

 WILDERNESS PRESS . . . *on the trail since 1967*

Walking Denver: 32 Tours of the Mile High City's Best Urban Trails, Historic Architecture, and Cultural Highlights

Second edition, first printing

Copyright © 2018 by Mindy Sink

Distributed by Publishers Group West
Manufactured in the United States of America

Cartography and cover design: Scott McGrew
Interior design: Lora Westberg
Photos: © Mindy Sink unless otherwise noted
Indexing: Rich Carlson

Library of Congress Cataloging-in-Publication Data

Names: Sink, Mindy, author.
Title: Walking Denver : 32 tours of the Mile High City's best urban trails, historic architecture, and
    cultural highlights / Mindy Sink.
Description: Second edition. | Birmingham, Alabama : Wilderness Press, [2017] | "Distributed by
    Publishers Group West"—T.p. verso. | Includes index.
Identifiers: LCCN 2017044547| ISBN 9780899978680 (paperback) | ISBN 9780899978697 (ebook)
Subjects: LCSH: Walking—Colorado—Denver—Guidebooks. | Hiking—Colorado—Denver—
    Guidebooks. | Denver (Colo.)—Guidebooks.
Classification: LCC GV199.42.C62 S755 2017 | DDC 796.5109788/83—dc23
LC record available at https://lccn.loc.gov/2017044547

Published by 🐾 **WILDERNESS PRESS**
              An imprint of AdventureKEEN
              2204 First Ave. S., Suite 102
              Birmingham, AL 35233
              800-443-7227, fax 205-326-1012

Visit wildernesspress.com for a complete list of our books and for ordering information. Contact us at
our website, at facebook.com/wildernesspress1967, or at twitter.com/wilderness1967 with questions
or comments. To find out more about who we are and what we're doing, visit blog.wildernesspress.com.

Cover photo: City Park with the Denver syyline and Rocky Mountains in the distance (Walk 15, page 82);
Russell Kord/Alamy Stock Photo

Frontispiece: Cherry Creek Trail (Walk 7, page 36); courtesy of Visit Denver

SAFETY NOTICE: Although Wilderness Press and the author have made every attempt to ensure that
the information in this book is accurate at press time, they are not responsible for any loss, damage, in-
jury, or inconvenience that may occur to anyone while using this book. You are responsible for your own
safety and health while following the walking trips described here. Always check local conditions, know
your own limitations, and consult a map.

Acknowledgments

When I wrote the first edition of *Walking Denver*, I relied on experts from Visit Denver, Historic Denver, and other local resources. This time I relied on my previous work, taking a fresh look at everything on my walks. The most important difference for me on these walks was doing them with my daughter, Sophie Seymour, who wrote the "Kid Tips" in many of these chapters for the benefit of families who enjoy doing the walks. I am so glad she participated fully, and I'm grateful to my editors for taking a chance on having a kid coauthor this time.

Author's Note

With the mild climate and nearly year-round sunshine in Denver, you can enjoy a walk in any season here. And, yes, some of the walks reach that exact 5,280-foot mark above sea level here in the Mile High City (and higher when you get into the foothills). Keep that elevation in mind when out for a walk—especially if you are not a local—and always have water, sunscreen, and a hat. Even on a seemingly flat city walk, the altitude can be a factor, so be sure to rest often and stay hydrated. It's a good idea to wear layers when out for a walk too, as the day can start off chilly, then become hot quickly with the bright sun. Conversely, it can cool off fast when the sun goes down. In short, bring a backpack that you can keep loading and unloading during a walk.

I would never brag about my sense of direction, but at least I know that the mountains are always to the west when I'm in downtown and I can orient myself. Let them prevent you too from getting turned around while walking Denver—and enjoy the view!

—*Mindy Sink*

Walking Denver

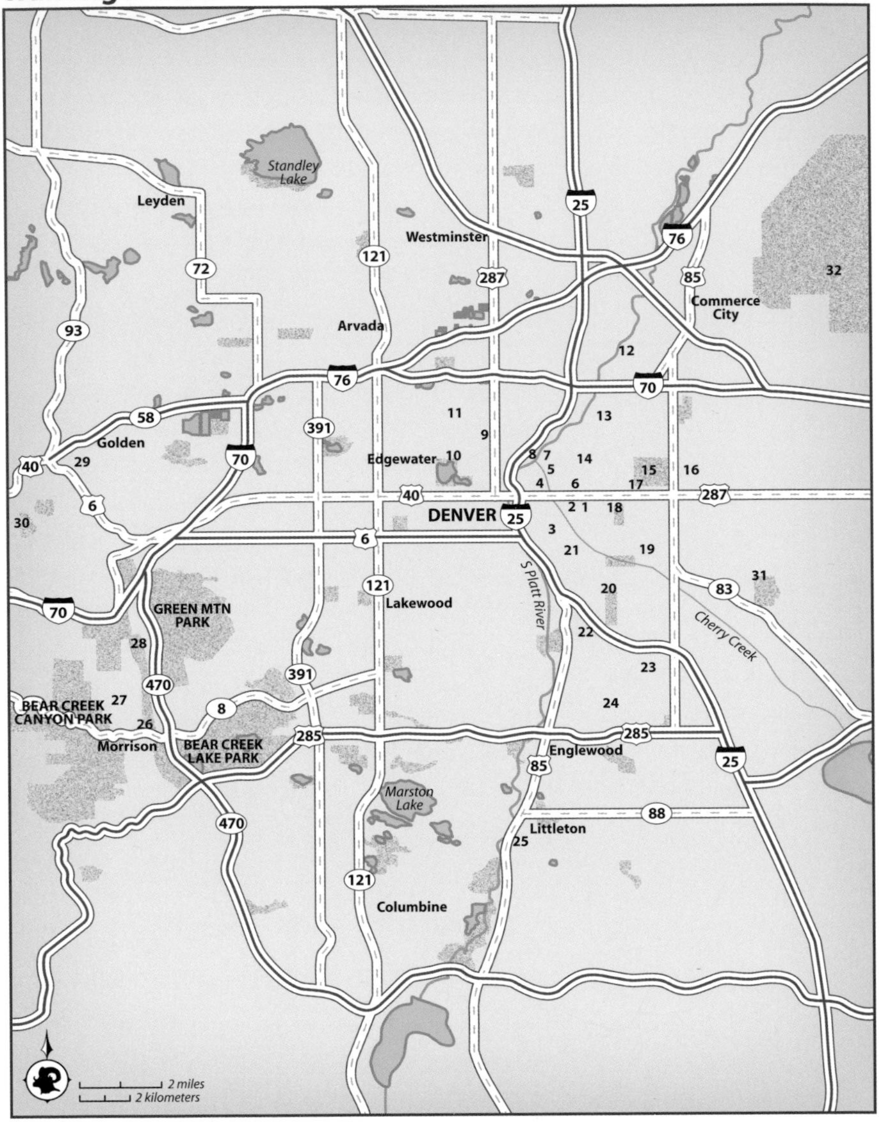
Standley Lake
Leyden
Westminster
Arvada
Commerce City
Golden
Edgewater
DENVER
Lakewood
GREEN MTN PARK
BEAR CREEK CANYON PARK
Morrison
BEAR CREEK LAKE PARK
Englewood
Marston Lake
Littleton
Columbine
S Platt River
Cherry Creek
2 miles
2 kilometers
1 2 3 4 5 6 7 8 9 10 11 12 13 14 15 16 17 18 19 20 21 22 23 24 25 26 27 28 29 30 31 32

Numbers on this overview map correspond to walk numbers. A map for each tour follows the text for that walk.

Table of Contents

Introduction

Denver is a compact city that is great for walking around, and it is also surrounded by some wonderful places worthy of walks that can feel like a little vacation.

This book was written with the idea that many of these walks can be combined—to possibly explore adjacent neighborhoods or to simply make for a longer walk on a beautiful day. The really ambitious pedestrian could connect the first 11 walks, or take one walk and then after a short light-rail train ride, take another walk too.

Although Denver has the 10th largest downtown in the country, that area is so compact that within a one-mile radius you can walk to a majority of the Mile High City's historic, architectural, and cultural highlights.

Beyond the appeal of the city itself are some intriguing towns and places to explore—each with a strong connection to Denver, such as a prolific architect, a city that was once the state capital, or a terrific view of Denver itself.

It's not just that there is a lot to see and do in Denver for locals and tourists alike, but also that those sites or towns are best enjoyed on foot, when you can soak up the Colorado sunshine almost every day of the year, smell the pine trees, see the whimsical or historical public art, and stop in for a bite to eat along the way.

1 Capitol Hill:
Politics and Architecture Rolled into One

Above: Tour the Molly Brown House Museum. See page 6 for more about Molly Brown.

BOUNDARIES: Colorado State Capitol Building, 14th Ave., Pennsylvania St., Governors' Park, Logan St., Colfax Ave.
DISTANCE: 2.25 miles
DIFFICULTY: Easy
PARKING: Metered on-street parking is available along Sherman St., which intersects State Capitol Building, and on Grant St. on the east side.
PUBLIC TRANSIT: Denver B-cycle (denverbcycle.com) has nearby bicycle rental stations at 13th Ave. and Pennsylvania St., 12th Ave. and Sherman St., and elsewhere. RTD buses (rtd-denver.com) serve this area.

Denver's Capitol Hill neighborhood offers a peek into the city's earliest years and how the boom and bust cycles affected even just a few blocks, as castle-like mansions went up and then fell into disrepair when apartment buildings were built next door. Once homesteaded land beyond the muddy streets of downtown, this little slope was soon recognized for its views of the mountains and remove from the noise and chaos of city life. In 1868, Henry C. Brown (owner of the Brown Palace Hotel) donated his acreage for the capitol building—only to take it back and put grazing livestock on it when the construction did not begin as soon as he had wanted it to. A lawsuit secured the land rights, and the grand structure was completed in 1908. Meanwhile, many of the city's wealthiest citizens had mansions built in the vicinity, only to have to sell them after the Silver Crash of 1893. J. J. Brown, husband of the "Unsinkable" Molly Brown (no relation to Henry C. Brown), moved into the neighborhood in 1894. (He made his fortune in gold and copper.) The couple made their mark on Capitol Hill and Denver with their wealth and charity, and on this walk you'll see their former home as well as other institutions they funded. Today the Capitol Hill neighborhood is a hybrid of architectural elements with Art Deco apartments, beautifully restored historic homes and churches made from stone and brick, high-rise buildings, and other curiosities.

Walk Description

Begin this walk on the mile-high step of the west side of the ❶ Colorado State Capitol Building. Confused yet? You should be. There are no fewer than three mile-high markers on these steps, thanks to advances in technology for making accurate measurements and the shifting ground below. Pick your favorite step (I like the one carved with the words "One Mile Above Sea Level") and enjoy the view to the west looking out over statues, monuments, Civic Center Park, the historic Denver City and County Building, and, finally, the Rocky Mountains. Free weekday tours of the Capitol Building tell visitors about the Colorado materials used in the building's construction as well as murals and stained glass portraits. Heartier walkers can even climb up inside the golden dome.

Facing west on the steps, turn left and exit the parking lot before crossing Sherman Street and cross 14th Avenue.

Turn left again and cross Sherman Street to begin walking east up 14th Avenue. The grand building to your right was the first home of the Colorado State Museum and was designed by architect Frank Edbrooke in 1915. It now serves as an annex for state offices. Also on your right is the ❷ First Baptist Church of Denver, whose congregation was founded in 1864 prior to the statehood of Colorado. The landmark historic building was constructed in 1936 and boasts a remarkable—and also historic—pipe organ.

Continue walking east up 14th Avenue, crossing first Grant Street, then Logan Street, and then Pennsylvania Street.

Immediately after crossing Pennsylvania Street, take a right and walk south on Pennsylvania Street. On your left is what started out as the St. Mary's Academy Building in 1911—in part built here to be in proximity to one of the Catholic girls' school benefactors, Molly Brown. After being used as offices for Woolworths and other entities, then converted to condominiums, the building is today a regional headquarters for the Salvation Army.

Just up the street is the former home of Molly Brown herself at 1340 Pennsylvania Street. Tours of the ❸ **Molly Brown House Museum** are available (walk around to the carriage house in the rear to make a reservation) and recommended to learn more about the full life of this remarkable woman. Molly Brown spent much of her adult life traveling for long periods of time abroad and rented this house out, even to a sitting governor for one year.

At the corner of 13th Avenue and Pennsylvania Street is the old Penn Street Garage, where Molly Brown once stored her own (electric!) car. This 1911 building was a working service garage until 1997, when it was converted to restaurants and lofts. Stop in at ❹ **Pablo's Coffee** if you need some caffeine to keep you going.

If it's a hot summer day, look forward to welcome shade for the next several blocks of the walk.

Just before crossing 12th Avenue, the ❺ **Capitol Hill Mansion Bed and Breakfast Inn** will be on your right. Built in 1891 in the Queen Anne style, the mansion was a private home for many years, and then turned into a hotel, private apartments, offices, a convalescent home, and finally was renovated in 1993 to become a luxurious bed and breakfast. You get a neighborhood feel with easy access to downtown amenities.

Cross 12th Avenue as you continue on Pennsylvania Street. The stunning condominium complex on the right started out as two separate homes in the 1890s that were joined in 1930 to become a nursing home. Today these are privately owned condos.

Cross 11th Avenue and you will be walking past a French Renaissance chateau mansion on the right. Built in 1891, the former home is rumored to be haunted with typewriters working by themselves, lights flickering, and other bizarre happenings over the years. Today guests of the ❻ **Patterson Inn** can decide for themselves if this is an otherworldly experience.

Cross 10th Avenue, then 9th Avenue, and then 8th Avenue, walking past the No Outlet sign (just for cars). On your right is the ❼ **Governor's Residence at Boettcher Mansion,** which was built by the Cheesman family in 1908 and then sold to businessman Claude K. Boettcher in 1923. The Boettcher family filled the already-grand house with furnishings and artwork from their international travels and remodeled some rooms before donating the home to the state. It is open for free tours on select days each year. (Not every governor chooses to live in the mansion; Governor Bill Owens never moved his family there during his two terms from 1999 to 2007, and current governor John Hickenlooper did not move into the mansion when he took office in 2011.)

Walk to the end of this very short block and you will see the ❽ **Grant-Humphreys Mansion** on the left. James B. Grant was the third governor of Colorado and had the 30-room mansion built in 1902. Albert E. Humphreys, a successful entrepreneur, bought it in 1911 from Grant's widow. Today it is used for private functions such as weddings.

Follow the sidewalk south as it becomes a path into ❾ **Governors' Park.** As you wind down the path, pause on the hilltop to get a glimpse of the mountains to the south. This gives you a sense of how grand the views are from the Governor's Mansion's Palm Room. There is a playground here for little tikes to enjoy.

Turn right at the bottom of the second staircase and follow the path until it joins with the sidewalk, and continue right. One of Denver's premier restaurateurs, Frank Bonanno, has two places to choose from for dinner only a block away: ❿ **Luca d'Italia** and ⓫ **Mizuna.** Walk north on Logan Street with the Governor's Mansion on your right.

Cross 8th Avenue, and keep walking north on Logan Street. Cross 9th Avenue, and on your left is the back of the Colburn Hotel and Apartments with ⓬ **Charlie Brown's Bar & Grill** on the ground floor. The Colburn was made semifamous when Jack Kerouac and Neal Cassady hung out there in 1947, when Cassady's future wife lived there. Before that time, architect J. J. B. Benedict (see Walk 25) had lived at the Colburn after leaving Littleton. Stop in at Charlie Brown's for a drink, and enjoy the live piano music in this neighborhood bar.

Cross 10th Avenue. On your right at 1030 Logan Street will be a rare Spanish Colonial Revival mansion, which was built in 1896.

Cross 11th Avenue and then 12th Avenue. On your right is quite a surprise amid the stone mansions and high-rise apartment buildings of this neighborhood   a wood-frame cottage built in 1886. It is rare to find wood-frame houses of this vintage since building codes in the 1880s required brick only after several large fires damaged many structures in town.

Cross 13th Avenue. On your left is a precious single building, the home of the ⓭ **Denver Woman's Press Club,** on the left, where the tiny brick building built in 1910 sits alone between giant asphalt parking lots on either side. Molly Brown was an early member of the club—one of the wealthy patrons brought on to attract new members. On your right you will notice the ⓮ **Starkey International Institute for Household Management,** which is a school for maids and butlers—just like the ones that perhaps once worked in this home when it was owned by a prominent social couple in the early 1900s.

Cross 14th Avenue and walk one block to Colfax Avenue. You will see the ⓯ **Cathedral Basilica of the Immaculate Conception** directly across the street. Once again, J. J. and Molly Brown figure in to the story: the Catholic couple joined with other investors to purchase the land for

Backstory: Unsinkable and Unforgettable Molly Brown

The Unsinkable Molly Brown, as she is best known for surviving the sinking of the *Titanic* in 1912, first came to this house on Pennsylvania Street when the owners lost their fortune in the Silver Crash of 1893. Her husband, J. J. Brown, made his fortune in gold and copper mines in Leadville, Colorado, and they enjoyed many years of prosperity together. Even after the couple separated, Molly Brown kept the house and would rent it out when she traveled. But the hard times of the Depression forced her to turn it into a boarding-house. The house was sold after her death in 1932 and turned into 12 separate living spaces. By the 1970s, the neighborhood had drastically declined and the house with it, so it was likely next up for the bulldozer as urban renewal enthusiasts came through. The home's owner appealed to Ann Love, wife of then governor John Love, and she rallied supporters to create Historic Denver and saved the house of the famous Molly Brown. The fledgling nonprofit was able to restore the home to its more glamorous heyday.

Today the work of Historic Denver is seen throughout this neighborhood and many others. Their series of architectural guides offers greater detail on many of the homes and buildings given historic designation. And, of course, these guidebooks are sold at the Molly Brown House Museum.

this cathedral in 1902. The building was completed in 1912. Pope John Paul II read mass here for World Youth Day in 1993.

Turn left and cross 14th Avenue as you walk west on Colfax Avenue. On the east side of the State Capitol Building you can see the public-art statue *The Closing of an Era,* which depicts a Native American man standing by a slain bison.

Cross Grant Street and continue down Colfax Avenue to cross Sherman Street. Immediately after crossing Sherman Street, take the smaller sidewalk that veers left as a path under the crab apple trees.

The path leads to the Civil War Monument where this tour ends. Don't worry about those Civil War–era cannons on either side—they were capped after the 21-gun salute ended with someone's clothes catching fire during a 1935 Colorado Day celebration.

Points of Interest

1. **Colorado State Capitol Building** 200 Colfax Ave., 303-866-2604, colorado.gov
2. **First Baptist Church of Denver** 1373 Grant St., 303-861-2501, fbcdenver.org
3. **The Molly Brown House Museum** 1340 Pennsylvania St., 303-832-4092, mollybrown.org

Capitol Hill

4 Pablo's Coffee 1300 Pennsylvania St., 303-832-1688, pabloscoffee.com

5 Capitol Hill Mansion Bed and Breakfast Inn 1207 Pennsylvania St., 800-839-9329, capitolhillmansion.com

6 Patterson Inn 420 E. 11th Ave., 303-955-5142, pattersoninn.com

7 Governor's Mansion at Boettcher Residence 400 E. 8th Ave., 303-866-5344, colorado.gov/governor/residence

8 Grant-Humphreys Mansion 770 Pennsylvania St., 303-894-2505

9 Governors' Park 701 Pennsylvania St., 720-913-1311

10 Luca d'Italia 711 Grant St., 303-832-6600, lucadenver.com

11 Mizuna 225 E. 7th Ave., 303-832-4778, mizunadenver.com

12 Charlie Brown's Bar & Grill 980 Grant St., 303-860-1655, charliebrownsbarandgrill.com

13 Denver Woman's Press Club 1325 Logan St., 303-839-1519, dwpconline.org

14 Starkey International Institute for Household Management 1350 Logan St., 303-832-5510, starkeyintl.com

15 Cathedral Basilica of the Immaculate Conception 1530 Logan St., 303-831-7010, denvercathedral.org

2   Civic Center Park and Golden Triangle:
Trifecta of Art, Politics, and Money

Above: *Daniel J. Libeskind designed the Frederic C. Hamilton wing of the Denver Art Museum.*

BOUNDARIES: Colfax Ave., Broadway, 11th Ave., Cherokee St.
DISTANCE: 1.5 miles
DIFFICULTY: Easy
PARKING: Metered parking is along many streets on this route.
PUBLIC TRANSIT: One block from RTD bus station at 16th and Broadway

Even Denver's earliest civic leaders sought to make the city attractive with parks and public art. On this walk the public art on display dates back as early as 1911 and includes outdoor murals painted in 1920 and bronze sculptures created in 1922 just steps away from modern pieces of fiberglass, marble, and steel made in this century. Civic Center Park was designed to be the city's heart—anchored by the most significant government buildings on the east and west axis and filled with classical architecture, trees, flowers, and monuments. The park has served as a staging ground for important political announcements and events and annually is used for public festivities such as the Taste of Colorado and Cinco de Mayo. As the Denver Art Museum has grown, so have the art galleries in the adjacent neighborhood, now called the Golden Triangle for its position between Broadway, Speer Boulevard, and Civic Center. The United States Mint at Denver near the end of the tour is an opportunity to see how money in circulation today may become tomorrow's artifacts.

Walk Description

Begin on the steps of Voorhies Plaza on the north end of ❶ **Civic Center Park,** near Colfax Avenue. Beginning in 1878, civic leaders sought to beautify Denver with tree-filled parks. The dreams for Civic Center Park that began in the late 1800s were fully realized over a thirty-year span, largely led by Mayor Robert Speer, who was a champion of the City Beautiful movement. The buildings and statues reflect the neoclassical architecture and Beaux Arts style favored at the time. Businessman John H. P. Voorhies, who lived across the street from where the park is now, funded the Voorhies Memorial. Look up to see the murals painted by artist Allen T. True.

Walk south out of the plaza and around the Children's Fountain with two cherubs frolicking on sea lions, which spout water at each other in the summer (kids, it's tempting in summer, but the rules say not to get in this water). On your right you will notice a small water fountain dedicated to Emily Griffith, who started the Opportunity School for students of all ages and backgrounds in 1916 just a few blocks from here (the school survives to this day as the Emily Griffith Technical College at 1860 Lincoln Street, not far from the beginning of this walk). Nearby is the ❷ **McNichols Building,** which was the first building on the Civic Center Park site in 1909 when it debuted as the Carnegie Library. After use as office space for decades, the building was renovated for use as exhibition space for the city's first Biennial of the Americas in 2010. As you walk into the center of the park, there is a bronze sculpture of Christopher Columbus to the left. This artwork by William F. Joseph was installed in 1970 and has sometimes angered Native Americans who protest on Columbus Day. In spring and summer the flowerbeds are filled with colorful blossoms in full bloom. From the middle of the park you can look left to see the gleaming golden dome of the ❸ **Colorado State Capitol Building** on what was once just called "Brown's Bluff." Between the Capitol Building and Civic Center Park you will also see the 1990 Colorado Tribute to Veterans Monument made of Colorado red sandstone. To the east is the ❹ **Denver City and County Building,** which is dressed up with bright lights and holiday displays December through mid-January (until the end of the annual National Western Stock Show). As you approach the park's south end you will see two bronze sculptures representing different aspects of early Western life: *On The War Trail* (1922) and *Bronco Buster* (1920), both by artist Alexander P. Proctor.

The Denver City and County Building is lit up for a festive event. *photo courtesy of Visit Denver*

Walk up the stairs into the Greek Theatre, which is used for cultural and political events. Don't miss the large murals painted by Allen T. True in the archways on either side of the structure's middle. These fragile murals were originally painted in 1920 and have since been restored.

Cross the 14th Avenue Parkway as you leave the park. To the left is the **❺ Denver Public Library,** designed by architect Michael Graves. Just outside the children's section is the playful sculpture *The Yearling* (2003) of a horse on a large red chair by artist Donald Lipski. Beyond the miles and miles of books, the library also has an impressive Western art collection on display on the fifth floor, where history buffs can also delve into historical tomes and photographs in the Western History and Genealogy Department. On the seventh floor is the Vida Ellison Art Gallery, which not only shows off contemporary art monthly but also has a balcony with a lovely city view. To the right is the **❻ Denver Art Museum's north wing**—the Gio Ponti–designed building that opened in the 1970s. The red steel sculptures out front on the lawn are collectively called *Wheel* (2005) by Edgar Heap of Birds and are in part a reminder of the Sand Creek Massacre. Between the library and the museum is the painted steel sculpture *Lau Tzu* (1995) by artist Mark di Suvero; this piece is actually part of the museum's collection.

Kid Tip: If you don't get a chance to stop inside the library or the museum during this walk, there is a sculpture just outside the library and museum on the plaza you might be able to take a quick break at and climb the bars, as I did on this walk.

Cross 13th Avenue, and as you look to the west you will notice the skybridge that connects the Ponti building with the museum's newer wing, the Frederic C. Hamilton Building. Designed by architect Daniel J. Libeskind and opened in 2006, this part of the museum is like a piece of art itself. The sculpture *Big Sweep* (2006) by Claes Oldenburg and Coosje van Bruggen sits directly outside the door of this titanium-clad structure (note: there's a sign discouraging climbing on this art, so resist temptation). To the left are the Museum Residences, lofts also designed by Libeskind that sit atop the parking garage for the museum. Beverly Pepper's gigantic aggregate sculpture, *Denver Monoliths,* sits to the east of the museum. Mad Greens is a popular place for soup, salad, or sandwiches in this neighborhood. As you exit this Cultural Center Complex, you will pass the enormous bronze sculpture *Scottish Angus Cow and Calf* (2001) by artist Dan Ostermiller.

Cross 12th Avenue as the plaza becomes Acoma Street, and continue walking south. One block east at 12th and Broadway is the ❼ **History Colorado Center.** Inside are "time machines," a recreated Colorado town, a ski jump, and much more to let visitors experience the Centennial State's history. Just ahead on Acoma Street is the old Evans School, a 1904 building that is in the National Register of Historic Places. The three-story building sat empty for decades after the school closed and has been converted to lofts.

Cross 11th Avenue and note the ❽ **Curious Theatre Company,** just across Acoma Street on the left. The theatre is housed in an 1880 church building, and the company puts on five main-stage shows per year.

Turn right on 11th Avenue, and walk one block to cross Bannock Street.

Walk one more block to Cherokee Street, and turn left.

Walk south to the ❾ **William Havu Gallery** at 1040 Cherokee Street. This gallery represents a number of Colorado's best artists as well as others from around the country. Shows here range from photography to sculpture to painting.

Turn right to cross Cherokee Street and walk north to ❿ **Walker Fine Art,** an immense gallery space on the ground floor of a new high-rise building. The large space accommodates equally large artwork and installations. On the corner of this building is Metropolis Coffee, a popular neighborhood hangout for the caffeine crowd.

Cross 11th Avenue, and walk north on Cherokee Street. At 12th Avenue note that one block away is the restaurant ⓫ **Cuba Cuba** on Delaware Street. Two brightly colored historic houses have been joined to make for a delectable Caribbean dining experience that is a local favorite.

Turn right after crossing 12th Avenue, and cross Cherokee Street to walk east on 12th Avenue one block to Bannock Street. At the time of this writing, the ⓬ **Kirkland Museum of Fine & Decorative Art** was being moved—literally—from its original home in the Capitol Hill neighborhood to 12th Avenue and Bannock Street. Vance Kirkland was a local artist and art professor who had a small studio that was turned into a museum by one of his former students in 1996. In addition to Kirkland's studio, the museum is home to a treasure trove of international decorative art and Colorado and regional art, all in a salon-style display. (No one under age 13 is allowed in the museum, and visitors ages 13–17 must be accompanied by an adult.)

Turn left at Bannock Street, and walk one block to 13th Avenue. On your right is the ⓭ **Clyfford Still Museum,** which celebrates the rarely seen works of the reclusive abstract painter. The building itself is an architectural masterpiece by Brad Cloepfil of Allied Works Architecture to enjoy while wandering the galleries.

Cross 13th Avenue. On your left is the Native American Trading Company, a jewelry and art shop featuring Native American artisans. Next door on 13th Avenue is Pint's Pub, a very British-style bar and restaurant—which is obvious from the flag of England out front.

To the right at this intersection is the ⓮ **Byers-Evans House**—a real surprise practically under the eaves of the ultramodern Denver Art Museum. William Evans, son of the Colorado Territory's second governor, John Evans, was the second owner of this 1883 house, and his daughter lived there until 1981. Tours show off the original furnishings and tell of how the neighborhood changed around the house over 100 years.

Walk north on Bannock Street, and cross 14th Avenue. This time, the City and County Building will be on your left and Civic Center Park on your right. There are more Allen T. True murals to see inside the City and County Building (this neoclassical Beaux Arts building opened in 1932) and a few other sculptures too. Straight ahead across Colfax Avenue you will see the Wellington E. Webb Municipal Building and the marble sculpture *East 2 West Source Point* by Larry Kirkland out front. There are several public artworks inside this building and around it to see as well.

Turn left when you reach Colfax Avenue, and walk to Cherokee Street. As you are walking west you will surely see the Rocky Mountains in the distance. Cross Cherokee Street, and you will find yourself in front of the ⓯ **United States Mint at Denver.** The 1906 building is an example of Italian-inspired Gothic Renaissance architecture, and this side of it is the original, with seven additions since that now take up the entire city block. You typically need reservations for a tour, and the entrance is on the Cherokee Street side by the gift shop. Mostly what you will see made here are pennies, but the history is surprisingly interesting.

Turn around and walk east on Colfax Avenue back to Bannock Street.

Cross Colfax Avenue, and turn right to walk around the east side of the Wellington E. Webb Municipal Building (see Walk 14). You will pass by the stone and marble sculpture *Building Blocks* (2003) by Robert Murase on your right as you approach 15th Street.

Cross 15th Street, and turn right. Cross Cheyenne Place and end the walk at the Pioneer Monument Fountain. Designed by artist Frederick Macmonnies in 1910, the original version featured a bare-chested Native American, but locals were outraged and it was changed to Kit Carson, an 1800s frontiersman and trapper.

Civic Center Park and Golden Triangle

Points of Interest

1. **Civic Center Park** 100 W. 14th Ave. Pkwy., 720-913-1311, denvergov.org
2. **McNichols Building** 144 W. Colfax Ave., 720-936-2999, mcnicholsbuilding.com
3. **Colorado State Capitol Building** 200 W. Colfax Ave., 303-866-2604, colorado.gov
4. **Denver City and County Building** 1437 Bannock St., 720-913-1311, denvergov.org
5. **Denver Public Library** 100 W. 14th Ave. Pkwy., 720-865-1111, denverlibrary.org
6. **Denver Art Museum** 100 W. 14th Ave. Pkwy., 720-865-5000, denverartmuseum.org
7. **History Colorado Center** 12th Ave. and Broadway, 303-866-3682, coloradohistory.org
8. **Curious Theatre Company** 1080 Acoma St., 303-623-0524, curioustheatre.org
9. **William Havu Gallery** 1040 Cherokee St., 303-893-2360, williamhavugallery.com
10. **Walker Fine Art** 300 11th Ave., 303-355-8955, walkerfineart.com
11. **Cuba Cuba** 1173 Delaware St., 303-605-2822, cubacubacafe.com
12. **Kirkland Museum of Fine & Decorative Art** 1201 Bannock St., 303-832-8576, kirklandmuseum.org
13. **Clyfford Still Museum** 13th Ave. and Bannock St., 720-865-4317, clyffordstillmuseum.org
14. **Byers-Evans House** 1310 Bannock St., 303-620-4933, coloradohistory.org
15. **United States Mint at Denver** 320 W. Colfax Ave., 303-405-4761, usmint.gov

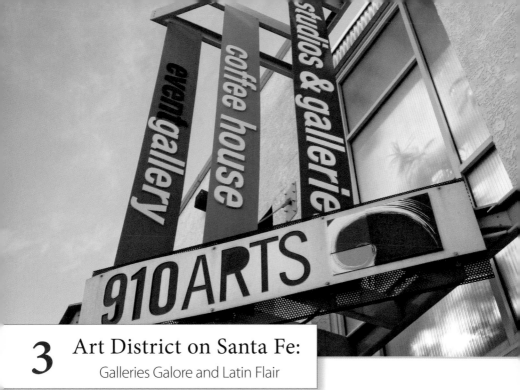

3 Art District on Santa Fe:
Galleries Galore and Latin Flair

BOUNDARIES: 7th Ave., Santa Fe Dr., 10th Ave.
DISTANCE: 0.5 mile
DIFFICULTY: Easy
PARKING: Free 2-hour parking is available on Santa Fe Dr. and side streets; $5 parking at West High School parking lot on First Fridays (proceeds fund the school's cultural programs) at 10th Ave. and Galapago St.
PUBLIC TRANSIT: The RTD light-rail stops at 10th Ave. and Osage St.; RTD 1 bus stops on this route.

The La Alma/Lincoln Park neighborhood of Denver is one with historic roots as deep as downtown and Auraria, but it remains lesser known. The buildings around here—whether homes, storefronts, warehouses, or theatres—date back to the late 1800s and turn of the century, and many have stucco covering the original brick, which gives more of a New Mexico feel than other parts of Denver. The primary business district of the neighborhood is along Santa Fe Drive, where you'll find the city's largest concentration of art galleries for three vibrant blocks. La Alma/Lincoln Park has a predominantly Hispanic population, and that culture resonates throughout a handful of the more significant galleries and art institutions on this walk. The emphasis in these art spaces is on local talent—artists based in Denver and Colorado—but there is also room for national and international work on display here. Even if you are not a serious art collector, the gift shops of some galleries make it easy for anyone to become a patron of the arts. On the First Friday of each month year-round, these narrow sidewalks are filled with people walking from gallery to gallery. During the holidays, traditional luminarias line the streets as well. Or it can be a fun afternoon stroll with a stop for tasty Mexican food and seeing art at your own pace.

Walk Description

Begin this walk on the west corner of 7th Avenue and Santa Fe Drive. Walk north on Santa Fe Drive. The majority of the galleries on this walk are members of Art District on Santa Fe— a collection of dozens of galleries, shops, and restaurants that goes beyond these three blocks. Along the walk you will see banners and window stickers for Art District on Santa Fe, and you can pick up very handy brochures with maps to guide you along this street and beyond.

On your immediate left is the Denver Civic Theater, now the home of ❶ **Su Teatro.** The building itself opened in 1921 as one of Denver's first silent movie theatres and had many other uses before renovation in the 1990s to be used as two theatre spaces. Su Teatro is the third-oldest Chicano theatre company in the United States. Su Teatro performs original plays, adaptations, and other works relevant to the Chicano/Latino community each year.

Next on this block is ❷ **Artists on Santa Fe,** a co-op gallery of Denver artists and their open studios where you can see them create ceramics, paintings, sculpture, and photography.

About halfway down the block after crossing 8th Avenue, step into ❸ **John Fielder's Colorado** gallery. John Fielder is Colorado's preeminent photographer, who is known for his vivid Colorado landscape images of mountain peaks, golden aspens, colorful wildflower meadows, and more. Fielder has published several books—guidebooks, children's books, instructional books—but may be best known for his *Colorado 1870–2000* books in which he recreates the landscape images of photographer W. H. Jackson. This gallery shows works of many other nature photographers too.

A few doors down is the ❹ **Museo de las Americas,** an educational space that also exhibits Latino art. The Museo is one of the organizations on Santa Fe Drive with a focus solely on Latino culture and art, through summer camps, workshops, and tours.

As you go to cross 9th Avenue, note that to your left is the **⑤ Renegade Brewing Company,** where you can sip fresh beer and talk with friends in their taproom—no TVs, on purpose!—and if you're lucky, there might be a food truck outside serving up a hot nibble.

Continuing on Santa Fe Drive after crossing 9th Avenue you will see the **⑥ Center for Visual Art** (the off-campus Metropolitan State University of Denver art gallery). Shows here go well beyond the student body art with exhibits by internationally recognized artists such as Christo and Jeanne-Claude, group shows by women artists from Vietnam and Japanese women ceramicists, all with educational components such as related workshops and lectures by visiting artists or professors.

At 10th Avenue, you can take a left and shop for some very hip ties at **⑦ Knotty Tie Co** (such a clever name!). Neck ties, bow ties, and pocket squares for the gents, lightweight scarves for the gals, all made right here in Denver.

If you missed the food truck at Renegade, pop into **⑧ Interstate Kitchen & Bar,** just across 10th Avenue, for some comfort food (brunch, lunch, or dinner on weekends, but just dinner on weekdays).

Although this walk doesn't continue north on Santa Fe Drive, it's worth noting that the Colorado Ballet relocated their headquarters to 11th Avenue and Santa Fe Drive in 2014, after decades at their previous location near the Capitol Hill neighborhood.

Pat Milbery's *Love This City* murals decorate the city.
photo courtesy of Visit Denver

Turn right again to walk south on Santa Fe Drive to return to 7th Avenue. The historic Aztlan Theatre will be on your left. It was built in the 1920s and is now used as a music venue.

Halfway down the block begins **⑨ 910 Arts,** which combines housing, exhibit, and performance space. The former livery and bottling plant space has an open-air courtyard, a coffee shop called Studio 6, eight lofts, and 17 studios, all of it painted in eye-catching bright yellows, reds, and greens.

At the corner of 9th Avenue is **⑩ Spark Gallery,** the Mile High

Backstory: The Whole Enchilada

The La Alma/Lincoln Park neighborhood is undergoing tremendous revitalization efforts, but because this development is occurring in somewhat isolated pockets of the greater area, walking may not be the best way to experience all of it. While much of this new growth in the area stems from light-rail lines and stops on the southern edge of the neighborhood, it is still not all pedestrian friendly. Another way to see the additional restaurants, breweries, galleries, and new lofts being converted from warehouses is to take the First Friday shuttle bus. The shuttle bus takes you from the light-rail train station at 10th Avenue and Osage Street by the Buckhorn Exchange—truly a sight itself with a large taxidermy collection on display on nearly every inch of wall space in Denver's oldest restaurant. The shuttle also brings people to this gallery walk between 7th Avenue and 10th Avenue on Santa Fe Drive. Find out more details at artdistrictonsantafe.com. This walk doesn't list every gallery or shop so that you can explore a bit and make discoveries. You'll find a mix of cultures, cuisine, art, and best of all, much of it locally made.

City's oldest art cooperative, featuring 30 established artists working in a variety of mediums, and the ⓫ **Core New Art Space** with shows by emerging artists.

Just after crossing 8th Avenue you will come to the ⓬ **CHAC (short for Chicano Humanities and Arts Council) Gallery & Cultural Center,** showcasing Latino/Chicano performance and visual art. Check their calendar for new visual artists, musicians, dancers, and poets, and plan ahead for their special events such as Santos & Crosses in August, El Dia de los Muertos in October and November, and Luminarias de la Guadalupe in December.

Surprise! Ethiopian food at Santa Fe Drive's ⓭ **Arada Ethiopian Restaurant** offers an alternative to the Mexican restaurants and pubs in the area with exotic dishes in a colorful dining room for dinner only.

Next up is what you expect in this neighborhood: simple and delicious Mexican food. ⓮ **El Noa Noa** has a courtyard with fountain and mariachi band for those warm summer nights in the city and simple combination platters or a la carte items with cold Mexican beer. Next door is ⓯ **El Taco de Mexico,** also with familiar beef or chicken tacos, of course, but adventurous eaters might want to try the tongue or brain on the menu in this small café.

At the corner of 7th Avenue and Santa Fe Drive, notice the Byers Branch Library. The Byers Library was built in 1918 as part of the Carnegie-funded libraries and is unique for its Spanish eclectic architectural style. The library was named for William N. Byers, founder of the now defunct *Rocky Mountain News,* and it is now a designated historic landmark.

The walk ends at 7th Avenue and Santa Fe Drive.

Art District on Santa Fe

Points of Interest

1. **Su Teatro** 721 Santa Fe Dr., 303-296-0219, suteatro.org
2. **Artists on Santa Fe** 747 Santa Fe Dr., 303-573-5903, artistsonsantafe.com
3. **John Fielder's Colorado** 833 Santa Fe Dr., 303-744-7979, johnfielder.com
4. **Museo de las Americas** 861 Santa Fe Dr., 303-571-4401, museo.org
5. **Renegade Brewing Company** 925 W. 9th Ave., 720-401-4089, renegadebrewing.com
6. **Center for Visual Art** 965 Santa Fe Dr., 303-257-1898, msudenver.edu/cva
7. **Knotty Tie Co** 926 W. 10th Ave., 303-954-9470, knottytie.com
8. **Interstate Kitchen & Bar** 1001 Santa Fe Dr., 720-479-8829, interstaterestaurant.com
9. **910 Arts** 910 Santa Fe Dr., 303-744-7979, 910arts.com
10. **Spark Gallery** 900 Santa Fe Dr., 720-889-2200, sparkgallery.com
11. **Core New Art Space** 900 Santa Fe Dr., 303-297-8428, coreartspace.com
12. **CHAC** 772 Santa Fe Dr., 303-571-0440, chacweb.org
13. **Arada** 750 Santa Fe Dr., 303-329-3344, aradarestaurant.com
14. **El Noa Noa** 722 Santa Fe Dr., 303-623-9968, denvermexicanrestaurants.net
15. **El Taco de Mexico** 714 Santa Fe Dr., 303-623-3926, eltacodemexicodenver.com

4 Auraria Campus:
The First Denver

BOUNDARIES: Champa St., 9th St., Auraria Pkwy., Speer Blvd.
DISTANCE: 1 mile
DIFFICULTY: Easy
PARKING: Fee parking lots
PUBLIC TRANSIT: RTD light-rail train stops at approx. Colfax Ave. and 9th St.

History can be so enlightening, just like a good education. Naturally there was more than one prospector around the confluence of Cherry Creek and the South Platte River in 1858. The town of Auraria was founded a few weeks before what became Denver City was settled on the other side of Cherry Creek. General William Larimer basically jumped a claim to secure Denver City for his party and then soon was in competition with the town founders of Auraria. As each city grew, and the discoveries of gold in the mountains lured more and more people to the area, the towns were united in 1860 (legend has it the unification was agreed to over a barrel of whiskey). One hundred years later, much of Auraria was gone and the site was filled with a 169-acre campus for three colleges: the Metropolitan State College of Denver, the University of Colorado at Denver, and the Community College of Denver. This walk threads through the historical buildings still standing and in use—Victorian cottages, churches, and a former brewery—amid the modern, bustling primarily commuter campus. As with many parts of Denver, this campus has been growing in recent years, so you will pass new buildings that may not be mentioned as they were under construction at the time of this writing.

Walk Description

Begin on 9th and Champa Streets at the east end of the Auraria townsite, also called the ❶ **Ninth Street Historic Park.** These 13 restored homes and former grocery store were built between 1872 and 1906. Walk west on either side of the grass divider between the houses. Although these charming Victorian-era homes are used as campus administrative office space today, small plaques in front of each house tell about the architectural style and who lived there originally. What makes this preserved block so appealing is how well maintained all of the houses are, including the individual fenced yards and gardens. It's as if the original residents might return to finish pruning the roses any minute and strike up a friendly conversation.

At the end of the block, turn right on Curtis Street. Walk under the skybridge between the campus buildings to the 10th Street Plaza, and keep going to the stone church ahead on the right.

Turn right in front of ❷ **St. Elizabeth of Hungary Roman Catholic Church** and walk east past the church to see the friary and shrine to St. Francis. The original church building became too small for the booming German, Irish, and other English-speaking parishioners, so it was torn down, and this building was erected in 1889. In 1908, the church became infamous when the pastor was murdered during morning communion. The monastery and courtyard were built in 1936. St. Elizabeth was one of three Catholic churches in a five-block area at Auraria, and only two were preserved during urban renewal efforts of the 1960s (St. Leo's was demolished). This church was completely renovated inside in the 1960s, including the stained glass windows you see today.

Walk back to the western corner of St. Elizabeth's and turn left. Walk south to the 10th Street Plaza again.

Golda Meir House

Turn right on the 10th Street Plaza. Just past the Lawrence Street Pedestrian Mall (which looks like a park to the left), you will see a very small stone building called the ❸ **Emmanuel Gallery.** Built in 1876 as an Episcopal chapel, this is Denver's oldest church structure. As the neighborhood around it changed, the church became a synagogue in 1903. It was sold, and from 1958 to 1973 the building served as an artists' studio for Wolfgang Pogzeba; in 1969 it was listed on the National Register of Historic Places. In 1973 the church became part of the Auraria campus and has functioned as an art gallery since that time. It's as tiny on the inside as it looks from the outside—a mere 24 feet by 66 feet. The gallery is open during typical business hours, so chances are you can go inside during this walk.

Continue walking west on the 10th Street Plaza to the Tivoli Commons. In the near distance (or rather, blocking your view of the mountains from this vantage point) is the Pepsi Center. Sitting on 52 acres of the Central Platte Valley, the Pepsi Center opened in 1999 as a state-of-the-art facility for concerts and sporting and political events. Both the Colorado Avalanche hockey team and the Denver Nuggets basketball team play here, and the 2008 Democratic National Convention was held here. (And, it should be noted, the views of the city skyline and the Rocky Mountains are spectacular from six-story atriums inside the Pepsi Center.)

But practically right in front of you now is the ❹ **Tivoli Center.** If you step inside this landmark-designated building you will quickly sense that it is comprised of 12 original structures (read: it's like a maze). As early as 1859, Denver had its first brewery, and by 1861 John Good was co-owner of the Rocky Mountain Brewery. In 1870 German-born Moritz Sigi began construction of the Tivoli Center, then called Colorado Brewery. After Sigi's untimely death, Good and another investor bought Colorado Brewery, changed the named to Milwaukee Brewery, and expanded with an opera house, tower building, a bottling company, and more at the site. By 1901 Good was the sole owner and changed the name to Tivoli, after the famous Denmark amusement park, then merged with the neighboring Union Brewery. The Tivoli-Union brewery even survived the Prohibition years by making a nonalcoholic beer called Dash. In the 1960s the name was changed to Denver Beer, and a few years later the brewery closed its doors for a decade. In the 1980s developers restored the buildings to their former glory with shows in the old opera house, restaurants, and added a three-story atrium to bind the once-separate historic buildings.

In the 1990s it was mostly converted to a student union but has since also returned to being . . .
⑤ Tivoli Brewing Company!

At this point in the walk, you can begin to loop back by turning left (see directions in next paragraph), or I recommend seeing more of the campus that features many of the newer buildings. As you walk west in the front of the Tivoli Student Union the **⑥ Tivoli Quad** is to your right. Take a right at Walnut Street, keeping the Tivoli Quad on your right. On your left is the **⑦ Marriott Hotel and Metropolitan State University of Denver Hotel and Hospitality Learning Center.** If you stay at the SpringHill Suites by Marriott here, you will be part of the classroom. Everyone working here is learning how to work in the events and hospitality business. When you are ready to turn back, head east on 12th Street to Larimer Street, follow it to 9th Street, and resume instructions below.

Turn left and walk to the 9th Street Plaza. This might be the best spot on this walk to look west for a view of the Rocky Mountains, especially at sunset. You will also see the curved outline of Invesco Field at Mile High, the home of the Denver Broncos, to the left of this view. Also note that the Tivoli Commons connects to Larimer Street going north (or right), Cherry Creek, and Larimer Square.

Turn left to walk east on the 9th Street Plaza to **⑧ St. Cajetan's Church,** the first Hispanic parish in Denver that dates to 1925. Thanks to funding from a wealthy Irishman, the church was built on this site near his old home. The Hispanic community grew around this church with a school, credit union, and clinic, only to be pushed out in the 1960s and 1970s. All but the church itself was razed, and it is used today as a theatre and conference center for campus functions.

As you pass St. Cajetan's, you will see two small homes on your right. The first is a rectory; the second is the relocated former home of Golda Meir. This house is out of place in more ways than one. This is the only remaining US residence of former Israeli prime minister Golda Meir. At age 15, Golda Meir ran away from home in Milwaukee to avoid an arranged marriage and continue her education. She came to Denver where her sister had already moved with her husband and child. Meir attended North High School in the Highlands neighborhood, while also working at her brother-in-law's laundry business. The small brick duplex was narrowly saved from demolition and moved twice before being saved and relocated to this site in the 1980s to preserve it. One half of the home shows off some of Meir's personal belongings and photographs of her, while the other is used as a conference center. Call 303-556-3292 to schedule a tour of the **⑨ Golda Meir House Museum.**

Walk east back to the Ninth Street Historic Park and down the other side of the grass divider to learn more about these houses and who lived here originally.

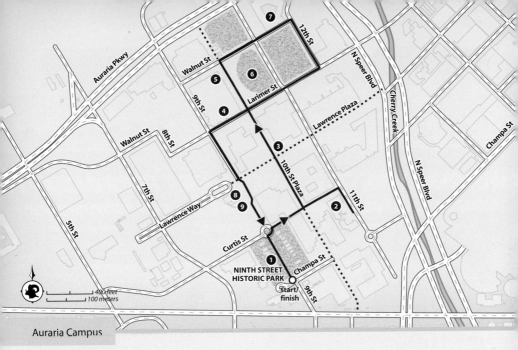

Auraria Campus

Points of Interest

1. **Ninth Street Historic Park** Auraria Campus

2. **St. Elizabeth of Hungary Roman Catholic Church** 1060 St. Francis Way, Auraria Campus; 303-534-4014; stelizabethdenver.org

3. **Emmanuel Gallery** 1205 10th St., Auraria Campus; 303-556-8337; emmanuelgallery.org

4. **Tivoli Center** Auraria Campus

5. **Tivoli Brewing Company** Auraria Campus, 720-458-5885, tivolibrewingco.com

6. **Tivoli Quad** Auraria Campus

7. **Marriott Hotel and Metropolitan State University of Denver Hotel and Hospitality Learning Center** 12th and Walnut Streets, msudenver.edu/hospitality

8. **St. Cajetan's Church** Lawrence Way, Auraria Campus; 720-556-3291

9. **Golda Meir House Museum** Auraria Campus, 303-556-3292, msudenver.edu/golda/house/museum

5 LoDo:
Saloons to Shops and Warehouses to Brewpubs

Above: Union Station anchors the Lower Downtown neighborhood.
photographed by Ellen Jaskol/Visit Denver

BOUNDARIES: 14th St., Larimer St., Wynkoop St., 22nd St.
DISTANCE: 1.75 miles
DIFFICULTY: Easy
PARKING: Metered parking on streets; fee parking lot on Market and 14th Sts.
PUBLIC TRANSIT: Market Street Station is 2 blocks away, and several RTD routes run through here;
    Denver B-cycle stations are nearby (denverbcycle.com).

Lower Downtown is likely Denver's most familiar historic district to locals and tourists alike, as it attracts office workers by day and revelers by night—and don't forget the baseball fans too. The very first buildings in the neighborhood likely burned or were flooded out, and after an 1863 ordinance required brick or stone, the next buildings became more permanent. The mighty warehouses, mercantile centers, and railway buildings withstood the elements, boom and bust economic cycles, and early urban "renewal" efforts to become today's lofts, offices, shops, restaurants, and bars in what is affectionately called LoDo by locals who are proud of this preserved corner of the Mile High City.

Walk Description

Start this walk on the southwest corner of ❶ **Larimer Square** at Larimer and 14th Streets. General William H. Larimer named this Denver City after the Kansas Territory Governor James W. Denver and in 1858 built a cabin on what is now his namesake block. Buildings were quickly built up in the area, and this block was filled with brothels, saloons, theatres, and the city's first bank and post office. In the 1960s, preservationist Dana Crawford (remember this name for when it appears later in this walk) and others stepped in and made sure that this historic block was saved. While most of these buildings date to the 1800s, there are also some much newer buildings squeezed in between. The Square is closed for annual events such as Chalk Festival in June. On the opposite corner is Tamayo, an upscale Mexican restaurant with a wonderful upper-deck patio that offers a view of the Rocky Mountains.

This block is filled with charming boutiques, but I'll let you explore and only call out one classic. Walk north on Larimer Street and stop in at Cry Baby Ranch, where cowboys, cowgirls, and little buckaroos can get the cutest T-shirts, boots, and accessories. So many restaurants, so little time! On this side of the street is Rioja, with inspired Mediterranean cuisine; the Market for coffee, sandwiches, and deli foods; Corridor 44, a champagne bar; and Osteria Marco, featuring family-style Italian food. On the opposite side of the street is Milk & Honey Bar, scrumptious American food for a full meal or quick snack with drinks, and down the Kettle Arcade courtyard you will find Bistro Vendôme, with a fine French menu. Every Christmas, Santa Claus greets children in this courtyard, and horse-drawn carriages take people on cozy winter rides around the neighborhood.

Cross 15th Street and turn left to walk west on 15th Street. Larimer Square is actually its own historic district, marked in part by the alley between Larimer and Market Streets. First cross Market Street, then Blake Street. At Wazee Street you will see the Wazee Supper Club, a great pizza place, on the opposite corner.

Turn right on Wynkoop Street. The old Colorado Saddlery Building on the corner is the largest of the warehouse buildings along Wynkoop Street. For the next few blocks you will find old loading docks in addition to sidewalks in front of these former warehouses.

These funky raised docks are one of your sidewalk options, but a fun remnant of the past. At the corner of 16th Street is the ❷ **Tattered Cover Bookstore** in the old Morey Mercantile

Building. On the 16th Street side you can see an old doorway on the second story that used to line up with the elevated 16th Street viaduct. There is a coffee and sandwich shop on the first floor of the bookstore.

The next block is the biggest change on this walk—and perhaps in this city—since this book was first published in 2011. At the northwest corner of 16th and Wynkoop Streets is a modern building with the Thirsty Lion restaurant on the ground floor. If you're a fan of giant TV screens and loud music, sit inside, but if like me you prefer a more natural setting, sit outside in the summer. Next up is ❸ **Union Station,** now housing the Crawford Hotel (yes, named after Dana Crawford) and many shops and restaurants.

Originally built in the 1880s, the train station has survived fires, renovation, and even the near end to railway transportation. Now it is the city's transportation hub and still a train station where you can buy a ticket to ride the rails to Los Angeles or Chicago and in winter the Ski Train to Winter Park. Just out the west doors is the subterranean entrance to a bus station, and above ground it's the gateway to light-rail trains, including the train to Denver International Airport. My favorite restaurants here include Mercantile (grab a fresh-squeezed juice to go) for sandwiches and salads, Snooze (plan ahead as there is always a line) for a calorific breakfast, and Milk Box Creamery (basically Little Man Ice Cream from Walk 8 under a different name). 5 Green Boxes is a delightful shop for a little gift, and there is a Tattered Cover here too. Oh wait, I almost forgot the bars! Head upstairs to the Cooper Lounge for a grand view of the Great Hall from above and a drink or just settle in at the Terminal Bar in the lobby and people watch. A giant Christmas tree is set up here during the holiday season, and it has become a favorite spot for families to get a picture for their holiday card. If it's summer, you might be here on the same day as the local farmers market that sets up on the plaza outside.

Kid Tip: About halfway through the walk, on the plaza outside of Milk Box Creamery at Union Station, there are some very cool fountains that you can splash in during the summer, spring, and sometimes early fall. While you have fun, your parents can sit on the stone slabs and relax for a bit while they watch you. Don't forget your swimsuit!

It's hard to leave this place, but back to the rest of the walk. The spot in front of Union Station and going east up 17th Street is the start of the annual National Western Stock Show parade, which begins with a longhorn steer cattle drive!

Heading north on Wynkoop Street, you'll notice that between 17th and 18th Streets are old warehouse buildings—once filled with supplies when the trains arrived across the street—shoulder to shoulder now turned into restaurants and other businesses. The most popular and well known of these restaurants is the ❹ **Wynkoop Brewing Company** at the 18th Street corner.

Sophie recommends the fountains at Union Station for some fun!

Billiards, dart lanes, their own Railyard Ale, and pub food are all available at the 'Koop (call 303-297-2700 to schedule a brewery tour). Colorado Governor John Hickenlooper (and former Denver mayor) was a founder of the Wynkoop and had a role in much of the transformation of these historic buildings.

Also at the corner of 18th and Wynkoop Streets is the Icehouse, a former creamery and cold-foods storage warehouse, now housing lofts and restaurants. The Old Map Gallery is housed here and so worth a visit for that one-of-a-kind gift or artwork for yourself.

At 19th Street and Wynkoop is the ❺ **Denver ChopHouse & Brewery** in the one-time Union Pacific Railroad Building—a place to spot all kinds of professional athletes, including the baseball players who play games right across the street. Here Wynkoop Street turns into a pedestrian plaza leading to ❻ **Coors Field,** home to Major League Baseball's Colorado Rockies team, at the northern end of the Lower Downtown Historic District. The public art archway, *The Evolution of the Ball* by Lonnie Hanzon, marks the entrance to Coors Field. It's fun to look at all the different types of silly balls on each side of the arch.

Cross over 20th Street on the overpass to Coors Field. Built in 1995, Coors Field was designed to match the historic warehouse buildings of the surrounding neighborhood. Special touches here include terra cotta columbine flowers (the state flower) and the purple mile-high row of seats that rings the nosebleed seats.

Turn right and walk east up the stairs and parallel to the baseball stadium. At the corner of 20th and Blake Streets, turn left to round the bronze statue *The Player* of baseball pioneer Branch Rickey. If you look one block east up 20th Street to Market Street, you will see the bar ❼ **El Chapultepec,** which has been serving libations since it was built in the late 1800s. Since the 1960s it has offered nightly jazz and was the place for big-name musicians (Mick Jagger, Branford Marsalis, Frank Sinatra, and many more) to stop in and jam when playing big gigs in Denver. The beer is cheap, the food is simple, and it's part of history.

Turn left on Blake Street to walk north alongside Coors Field. This east side of the baseball stadium is where to buy tickets, get souvenirs at the gift shop (assuming you really like purple!), stop in at the ❽ **Sandlot Brewery** (a Coors company, of course), and at the north end of the stadium check out the neon art of a baseballer sliding into home, *Bottom of the Ninth* by Erick C. Johnson.

Turn around and walk back to 20th Street, and cross the street to continue walking on Blake Street. It is sports bar mania along this block, but look closely and you will see there is a museum squeezed in too. ❾ **The National Baseball Museum** celebrates not just the Colorado Rockies but also the Bears (you just have to go inside to find out more) with seats, photos, cards, and other collectibles. On the right is ❿ **Falling Rock Tap House,** which gets mighty crowded in October during the Great American Beerfest thanks to the 70 or so beers to sample. Next door is the nightclub Beta for dancing all night long. Cross 19th Street, and the restaurants thin out a little. For dinner consider Vesta Dipping Grill or the 9th Door for Spanish-style tapas.

Turn right on 18th Street, and walk one block to Wazee Street.

Turn left at Wazee Street, and cross 18th Street. On the left is the ⓫ **Robischon Gallery,** an exceptional contemporary art gallery. If you cross 17th Street about midblock will be ⓬ **Rockmount Ranch Wear.** Owner Jack Weil invented the snap-front Western shirt and worked here every day until his death at age 107 in 2008. While the fancy cowboy shirts are worn by rock stars and rodeo riders, even the T-shirts make terrific souvenirs for just about anybody. Across the street is ⓭ **David Cook Fine Art;** here they combine Native American art with regional American art of the 19th and 20th centuries.

Cross Wazee Street, and walk back toward Union Station. On your left on 17th Street will be the lovely ⓮ **Oxford Hotel,** Denver's oldest operating hotel. Opened in 1891, the hotel was such a success that they opened an annex across the alley (now a spa upstairs, fitness center downstairs), and in 1933 opened the Art Deco Cruise Room bar. Remember Dana Crawford from the beginning of the walk? She is also responsible for revitalizing the Oxford Hotel many years ago.

End your walk back at Union Station.

Points of Interest

1. **Larimer Square** between 14th and 15th Sts., 303-534-2367, larimersquare.com
2. **The Tattered Cover Bookstore** 1628 16th St., 303-436-1070, tatteredcover.com
3. **Union Station** 1701 Wynkoop St., 303-534-6333, unionstationindenver.com
4. **Wynkoop Brewing Company** 1634 18th St., 303-297-2700, wynkoop.com
5. **Denver ChopHouse & Brewery** 1735 19th St., 303-296-0800, denverchophouse.com
6. **Coors Field** 2001 Blake St., 303-762-5437, colorado.rockies.mlb.com/col/ballpark
7. **El Chapultepec** 1962 Market St., 303-295-9126
8. **Sandlot Brewery** 2161 Blake St., 303-312-2553
9. **National Baseball Museum** 1940 Blake St., 303-974-5835, ballparkmuseum.com
10. **Falling Rock Tap House** 1919 Blake St., 303-293-8338, fallingrocktaphouse.com
11. **Robischon Gallery** 1740 Wazee St., 303-298-7788, robischongallery.com
12. **Rockmount Ranch Wear** 1626 Wazee St., 303-629-7777, rockmount.com
13. **David Cook Fine Art** 1637 Wazee St., 303-623-8181, davidcookfineart.com
14. **Oxford Hotel** 1600 17th St., 303-628-5400, theoxfordhotel.com

6 16th Street Mall/Downtown:
Made for Walking

Above: The historic clock tower is part of the 16th Street Mall.
photographed by Steve Crecelius/Visit Denver

BOUNDARIES: Broadway, Tremont St., 14th St., Market St.
DISTANCE: 1.25 miles
DIFFICULTY: Easy
PARKING: Metered parking is available on all streets (meters are free on Sundays).
PUBLIC TRANSIT: Free 16th St. Mall Shuttle Bus; RTD bus station terminals at each end of 16th St.
  Mall service several routes; Denver B-cycle station at Market St. Station (denverbcycle.com; no
  bicycles allowed on 16th St. Mall).

Downtown Denver is compact and easily walkable, and perhaps the most pedestrian-friendly
place of all is the 16th Street Mall. These 16 blocks are closed to vehicular traffic (not counting the
cross streets every block or the free shuttle buses that go from end to end all day) and make for

an easy stroll among shops, restaurants, and hotels. Better yet, just a block or two in either direction of the 16th Street Mall there are many of Denver's best hotels—both historic, renovated, and brand new—as well as public art, art collections, and other attractions.

Walk Description

Start at the Civic Center Plaza at 16th Street and Broadway. Walk north on Broadway and cross the actual 16th Street (not the mall portion).

At 17th Street, look right. Inside the lobby of this reflective high-rise at 1670 Broadway is a Dale Chihuly piece, titled *Colorado Wildflowers,* that was installed by a previous owner of the building.

Cross 17th Street, then turn left and cross Broadway.

Walk north on Broadway again as you walk along one side of the triangular-shaped ❶ **Brown Palace Hotel.** The Brown is Denver's most elegant historic hotel. It is named for the man who had it built in 1892, Henry C. Brown. The 230-room Brown has three restaurants—Ship Tavern, Palace Arms, and Ellyngton's—as well as Churchill Bar, a cigar bar. Oh, and there is a luxurious spa in the basement . . . somewhere near the *original* artesian well that still supplies water to the hotel. Did I mention the eight-story atrium with stained glass ceiling and decadent chandelier? The lobby below the atrium offers tea service, cocktails, live piano music, and more throughout the year. There's so much rich history that they have their own historian to give you a tour (by reservation). For starters, they might tell you that every US president except Calvin Coolidge has stayed here. The holidays are a magical time here, kicking off with an annual Champagne Cascade and lighting of the decorations (and champagne brunch to boot!), holiday teas (make those reservations months in advance), and more.

At Tremont Street you will see ❷ **Trinity United Methodist Church** across the street. The church's 200-foot spire is made from rhyolite, a volcanic rock from Castle Rock, Colorado, and inside they proudly show off an 1880s-era Roosevelt Organ. Historic tours of the church are offered regularly.

Turn left and walk around the National Western Stock Show bronze statue. You might be wondering what this statue is doing here. Each year during the National Western Stock Show, there is a parade—complete with cattle drive—that makes its way up 17th Street (in the middle of January, no less) and ends at the Brown Palace. And there is a long-standing tradition that the stock show's prize-winning steer is put on display in the hotel's lobby . . . during teatime.

Walking down Tremont Street with the Brown Palace Hotel on your left again, you can see the historic Navarre Building on the right. More is known about the past use of this building than the present. Built in 1889, it was a bordello, and rumor has it that an underground passage allowed men to sneak from the Brown Palace to the Navarre. It has also been a school and a hotel and now it is the ❸ **American Museum of Western Art**–The Anschutz Collection (sorry kiddos, age restrictions), and you'll need to have a scheduled tour to see the art.

Cross 17th Street, and note that four and five blocks down 17th Street, respectively, are the ❹ **Magnolia Hotel** in the fully restored Equitable Bank Building (at Stout Street), the ❺ **Hotel Monaco** in the 1917 Railway Exchange Building and the Art Moderne Title Building (at Champa Street), and the ❻ **Renaissance Denver Downtown City Center Hotel** in the former Colorado National Bank building built in 1915. If you liked the Allen Tupper True murals on Walk 2, be sure to circle back to step into the Renaissance, where there are 16 of his murals in the lobby.

But for this walk, turn left and walk one block to the 16th Street Mall, which was built in 1982. If you were to continue two blocks farther on Tremont Street you would see the ❼ **1882 Denver Firefighter's Museum** (open for tours), which is a big hit with little kids.

Turn right on the 16th Street Mall and cross Tremont Street to begin walking west on the mall. On your left is the Denver Pavilions, like a mall at the mall that opened in 1998. Within the two-block-long Pavilions mall are chain restaurants, shops, bowling, and a movie theatre. There is an exception here and it's the ❽ **I Heart Denver Store** on the second level. This locally owned store not only sells Colorado-made products but a percentage of sales also goes to the makers.

Just before the corner of Glenarm Place is Cook's Fresh Market, a gourmet deli and market with delicious sandwiches, salads, soups, and more. On the other side of Glenarm Place is the ❾ **Paramount Theatre,** which opened to great fanfare in 1930 and still proudly shows off its Art Deco style both inside and out. In an era when newspapers are struggling and Denver's original newspaper, *The Rocky Mountain News,* closed up leaving only the *Denver Post* daily, there is the living relic of the ❿ **Denver Press Club** nearby. The Denver Press Club is the oldest of its kind in the United States, opened in 1867, and has been in this building about two blocks away on Glenarm Place between 14th and 13th Streets since 1925.

Keep walking west on 16th Street. At Welton Street is the 1889 Masonic Building, which was nearly lost to a fire in 1985 and then renovated for offices, shops, and restaurants, such as the Appaloosa Grill.

As you approach California Street, stop in at Visit Denver on your right. Here you will find plenty of brochures, maps, guidebooks, and helpful advice. They might even direct you to the ⓫ **Dikeou Collection** across the street. Located on the fifth floor of the Art Deco Colorado Building, you would never guess there is office after office of wild contemporary art from artists around the world.

Turn left and walk south on California Street. On your left is a piece of public art, *Vacationland,* by artist Gary Sweeney (his art can be seen elsewhere in Denver, including at the airport). To your right is the Denver Dry Goods Building, built between 1889 and 1906 and home to the local retailer until the 1980s. It now serves many purposes as lofts, retail space, and offices. Across 15th Street is the Hyatt Regency, where Peaks Lounge on the 27th floor has fantastic views of the mountains.

As you approach 14th Street and the ⑫ **Colorado Convention Center,** you will see large public art on display—there is even more inside the center. Jonathan Bonner's *Stone Garden* invites people to sit and mingle outside the center. If it's cold out, see if you can go inside and take a ride on Jim Green's *Laughing Escalator.*

Turn right to walk west on 14th Street. By now you have already spotted *I See What You Mean,* or as most everyone calls it, the Big Blue Bear. Installed in 2005 by artist Lawrence Argent, the 40-foot-tall bear peeking in the convention center windows is by far the city's most popular and recognized public art. Miniature versions are sold in gift shops, such as at the Denver Art Museum.

After cautiously crossing Stout Street, where bell-clanging light-rail trains come through, walk to Champa Street. On the corner is the ⑬ **Denver Performing Arts Complex,** which started with the Municipal Auditorium in 1908 to host the city's first Democratic National Convention. That historic building is now home to the very modern Ellie Caulkins Opera House. There is a Dale Chihuly glass sculpture inside this theatre. Inside the complex are a handful of other theatres and public art. It's worth taking a detour through the soaring glass-and-steel open-air atrium to see it all. On the south side of the complex is a lawn where special events take place throughout the year, including a children's Shakespeare Festival. Jonathan Borofsky's *The Dancers* is an immense public art sculpture gracing this side of the theatre complex.

Return to 14th Street, and as you cross, look left (west). One block away on 14th and Arapahoe Streets is the ⑭ **Hotel Teatro,** a luxury boutique hotel that honors the theatre connection with photographs of past productions throughout. Walking with a pooch? Hotel Teatro is pet friendly!

At Curtis Street you'll see the *All Together Now* sculpture by artists Roberto Behar and Rosario Marquardt just outside of ⑮ **The Curtis** hotel and the Corner Office Restaurant and Martini Bar, both with hip retro touches in style.

Walk north to 15th Street. Look to your right, and one block east on 15th Street you will see the former Denver Gas & Electric Building, which features 13,000 light bulbs on the exterior. After you cross 15th Street make sure you walk over the easy-to-miss sidewalk grates that are actually a piece of brilliant public art, *Soundwalk,* by artist Jim Green. As you step on each grate, different sounds—a clucking chicken, a yodeling woman, subway cars, to name a few—play loudly. By now you will be back on the 16th Street Mall.

Cross over the mall and turn left to walk west again. On your left is the ⑯ **Denver Money Museum** in the Federal Reserve Bank of Kansas City—you can either schedule a guided tour in advance or take a free self-guided tour with reservations (closed weekends). On your right is the original Rock Bottom Brewery. In the center strip of the bus lanes are more pieces of functional public art—concrete and ceramic tile chessboards by artists Susan Wick and Doug Eichelberger.

At Arapahoe Street you will be just about face to face with the Daniels & Fisher Tower, which is locally called the D&F Tower. This Denver landmark was built in 1910 as part of the Daniels & Fisher Department Store, which was later razed. At the time it was built it was the tallest building west of the Mississippi River. The tower was converted to offices, and in the basement is **⑰ The Clocktower Cabaret,** a nightclub featuring burlesque. About the only time to go inside the tower (aside from the cabaret) is during a private event or the annual Doors Open Denver architectural tour (doorsopendenver.com) in spring.

Perhaps the city's most subtle "park" is also right in front of you. Yes, really. **⑱ Skyline Park** is a linear park that stretches from 15th Street to 18th Street along Arapahoe Street. It was considered a highlight of Modernist landscape architecture when it was created in the 1970s. Although the park has been altered from the original design, the geometric fountains are a special feature. In summer free movie nights are held in the park, and in winter you can go ice-skating.

Continue walking west on the 16th Street Mall. After crossing Lawrence Street you will see Writer Square on your left. This collection of galleries, restaurants, and shops leads to Larimer Square and into the Lower Downtown Historic District (see Walk 5).

Walk west on 16th Street, and next cross Larimer Street. Looking to your left you will see— depending on the season—strings of holiday lights or banners draped across the street marking Larimer Square.

Walk one more block west on 16th Street to Market Street and cross. In the historic building facing Market Street Station is Two-Fisted Mario's Pizza for all-day and into-the-late-night pizza fixes and Mario's Double Daughter's Salotto, a very cool bar with an almost-believable backstory. This walk ends at Market Street Station.

Points of Interest

① **The Brown Palace Hotel** 321 17th St., 303-297-3111, brownpalace.com

② **Trinity United Methodist Church** 1820 Broadway, 303-839-1493, trinityumc.com

③ **American Museum of Western Art** 1727 Tremont Pl., 303-293-2000, anschutzcollection.org

④ **Magnolia Hotel** 818 17th St., 303-607-9000, magnoliahotels.com/denver

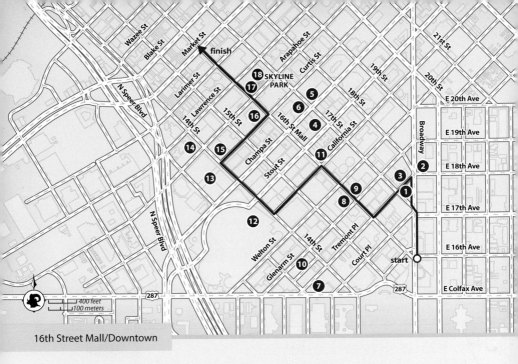

16th Street Mall/Downtown

5 Hotel Monaco 1717 Champa St., 303-296-1717, monaco-denver.com

6 Renaissance Denver Downtown City Center 918 17th St., 303-867-8100, rendendowntown.com

7 Denver Firefighter's Museum 1326 Tremont St., 303-892-1436, denverfirefightersmuseum.org

8 I Heart Denver 500 16th St. #264, 720-317-2328, iheartdenverstore.com

9 Paramount Theatre 1621 Glenarm Pl., 303-825-4904, paramountdenver.com

10 Denver Press Club 1330 Glenarm Pl., 303-571-5260, denverpressclub.org

11 Dikeou Collection 1615 California St. #515, 303-623-3001, dikeoucollection.org

12 Colorado Convention Center 700 14th St., 303-228-8000, denverconvention.com

13 Denver Performing Arts Complex 1101 13th St., 303-893-4000, denvercenter.org

14 Hotel Teatro 1100 14th St., 303-228-1100, hotelteatro.com

15 The Curtis 1405 Curtis St., 303-571-0300, thecurtis.com

16 Denver Money Museum 1020 16th St., 303-572-2300, kansascityfed.com

17 The Clocktower Cabaret 1601 Arapahoe St., 303-293-0075, clocktowercabaret.com

18 Skyline Park 1125 16th St.

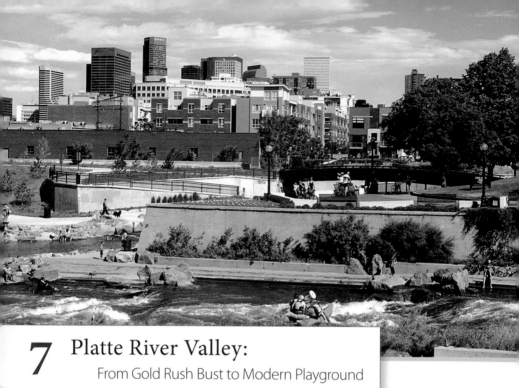

7 Platte River Valley:
From Gold Rush Bust to Modern Playground

Above: *Kayakers and others play in the South Platte River at Confluence Park.*
photographed by Stan Obert/Visit Denver

BOUNDARIES: Wewatta St., Cherry Creek, South Platte River, 19th St., Little Raven St.
DISTANCE: 2 miles
DIFFICULTY: Easy
PARKING: Free on-street parking for 2 hours is along Little Raven St.
PUBLIC TRANSIT: Denver B-cycle station on Little Raven St. (denverbcycle.com); light-rail train stops at Union Station half block from starting point on Wewatta St.; free RTD Mall Shuttle stops at Union Station.

Denver's Platte River Valley is exploding with development, energy, and an appreciation for the enduring history in this part of the city. Confluence Park is the birthplace of the Mile High City. In 1858, prospectors discovered a bit of gold along the South Platte River, just above the confluence with Cherry Creek, and it wasn't long after that the city of Denver was officially founded. Although the gold find turned out to be a bust, the town grew as a supply post and place for miners to escape from the harsh mountain winters where more substantial gold and silver mines were worked. The proximity to water in this arid land drew prospectors, Native Americans, and the earliest developers: John Brisben Walker opened the city's first amusement park, complete with medieval castle and riverboats, in 1887 on what is now Commons Park.

Today there are kayakers, sunbathers, and beachgoers frolicking in the waters of the confluence during summer's hottest days. As cyclists, joggers, pedestrians, and dog walkers navigate the paths alongside the creek and river, the grassy lawns of Commons Park are filled with people in fitness classes, playing a casual game of Frisbee or football, flying kites, and more in summer or sledding and skiing in the winter. Others are rolling along on skateboards or inline skates and headed for the ramps and bowls of the Denver Skatepark north of Commons Park.

Walk Description

Start on the northwest corner of 16th and Wewatta Streets on the eastern flank of the ❶ **Millennium Bridge,** and follow the sidewalk south as it curves around past Delgany Street. Cross 15th Street at the intersection and go right.

Walk one block west and cross Delgany Street, and you will find yourself at the entrance of the ❷ **Museum of Contemporary Art Denver.** Well, the entrance is in fact somewhat hidden in this black glass cube of modernism designed by architect David Adjaye (walk down the outdoor hallway and turn right to enter the museum). Inside, visitors will find the latest exhibitions, as well as a room for families to create art together and a rooftop café with local beer, coffee, and tasty foods.

Turn left and walk two blocks down Delgany Street to Cherry Creek. Turn right just before the footbridge and proceed down the ramp that merges with the footpath alongside Cherry Creek. (Note that there are paths on both sides of the creek: one designated for pedestrians, the other for bicyclers.) As you approach the confluence with the South Platte River, veer right and take the ramp up. Go right again when the ramp curves. At the top of the ramp, look left to see oversized granite sculptures of leaves and fishes by artist Andrew Dufford. Kids love to climb in and over these silly sculptures.

Turn right over the footbridge that spans Cherry Creek. The grass- and flower-covered hill on the other side is actually a landfill of garbage retrieved from the river's most polluted days in the 1960s. In summer this hill is packed with people enjoying free movie and concert nights.

Turn left off the bridge and walk until the path forks.

Take the right fork, staying somewhat straight until you are parallel with Little Raven Street. Walk under Speer Boulevard, where there are huge painted murals called ❸ *Confluent People* by artist Emanuel Martinez on both sides. The 10,000-square-foot murals show enormous faces of Denver's diverse population—with different ethnicities, genders, and ages represented—with much smaller figures reflected in the sunglasses on each face. Look for animals native to the South Platte River and Central Platte Valley in the mural also.

Turn right into ❹ **Centennial Gardens** just beyond the underpass. Centennial Gardens is modeled on French formal gardens but uses primarily native and drought-tolerant plants such as lavender, penstemon, juniper, and more. The gardens are typically open from 6 a.m. to 8 p.m., but this can vary when special events have the gardens reserved. The paths circle around splashing fountains, past neat hedgerows, and lead to shaded benches under a small pavilion.

After looping through Centennial Gardens, exit back onto Little Raven Street and turn left to walk north toward the Speer Boulevard underpass.

Just before the underpass, go left on the shared pedestrian and bike path. This short path ends at the South Platte River.

Turn right and walk under another section of Speer Boulevard as you walk north. When you come out from under the bridge, chances are you will feel the warm sun on your face any time of the year. With ducks and the occasional heron mucking about in the water below, it is easy to imagine how the natural and gentle beauty of this place drew people who had just crossed the dry plains or clambered down from the harsh mountains. Although it is like a crowded beach with children and adults splashing about with colorful inner tubes and water toys on hot summer days, signs do say not to get in the water here because of pollution.

Cross the first footbridge you come to on your left. As you cross the bridge, look to the southwest to see the Rocky Mountains and to the east to see the downtown skyline. If it's summer, you might see the Platte Valley Trolley waiting on the other side of the bridge, next to the flagship REI store. Back in 1871 the first horse-drawn trolley arrived in Denver, only to be replaced by cable cars, which in turn were replaced by electric trolley cars that took people all over the city. By 1950, cars and buses drove the trolley cars out of town. This historic "Breezer" trolley takes riders a short distance to the west, making stops at the ❺ **Downtown Aquarium** and the ❻ **Children's Museum of Denver,** which are also accessible on the bike and pedestrian path.

Kid Tip: Even if you don't have time to stop in the museum, there is still quite a fun array of quick, enjoyable activities just outside the museum and along the walk! The playground outside has places to climb, splash, and swing.

Turn right as you leave the bridge. On your right is a river overlook where you can stop and get pictures with the city skyline and ❼ **Confluence Park** as a backdrop. Here you will also see a large plaque that gives a detailed history of Cherry Creek and the South Platte River. Once these seemingly gentle waterways caused catastrophic floods before they were dammed, only to become severely polluted with toxic waste, cars, mattresses, and all kinds of garbage. Finally they were cleaned up in the 1970s to create the beautiful urban park you see today.

If you were to walk straight to 15th Street and turn left, you would find **❽ My Brother's Bar** for beer and burgers at both lunch and dinner. Brother's is one of Denver's oldest bars and made moderately famous because Jack Kerouac's pal Neal Cassady was a regular. Cassady's jailhouse note about settling his bar tab is on display there.

But save dining out for later, and now stay on the path that hugs the river. (This next section was under construction at the time of this writing but may be completed by the time you take this walk.) Turn right at the first ramp after the plaque and walk down as it zigzags parallel to the South Platte River. The ramp levels off on Shoemaker Plaza, named for Joe Shoemaker, the man credited with revitalizing Confluence Park. Continue walking north and follow the sign that points to **❾ Platte River Trail.** Stay on the sidewalk path as it zigs and zags a little more and goes under 15th Street.

Turn left to go up the stairs just after you walk under a footbridge spanning the river.

Turn left again at the top of the stairs and take the bridge east over the South Platte River. Often you can watch kayakers run the man-made rapids between Confluence Park and this bridge or see people playing with their dogs in the shallow water.

Follow the path as it curves gently to the left off the bridge. Then take a hard left at the base of the grassy hill.

Go right at the next juncture and head north. Often this is where the sounds of the river and birdsongs drown out the city noises. On your right you cannot miss the park's signature piece of public art, **❿ Common Ground** by artist Barbara Grygutis. This sculptural stone amphitheater is made from Colorado native lava rock. The staircase leads to a ramp that seems to merge with the path on the other side of the sculpture; it is meant to be walked in, so don't be shy.

Continue walking north as you pass the sculpture, keeping the river on your left. The sidewalk path continues north and then curves east to a juncture.

Go left at the juncture and walk north again, this time with flagstone walls, benches, and ornamental grasses to your right.

Commons Park ends at 19th Street across from the **⓫ Denver Skatepark,** where any day of the year there are skateboarders and rollerbladers sliding across the concrete bowls.

Kid Tip: So you left your board at home. As much as you might want to skate, it's still fun to watch other people show off their tricks.

Backstory: The Land of Peace Chiefs

The fact is, the land under our feet belonged to the Native Americans—specifically the Arapaho and Southern Cheyenne tribes—long before 1858. Approximately 1,500 Arapaho and Southern Cheyenne camped in the confluence area and lived off the buffalo that roamed these plains. When white men began coming to the area, Chief Little Raven told them to take all the gold, but remember the land belonged to the Native Americans. He and other chiefs who tried to coexist with the settlers were called the Peace Chiefs because they did not advocate bloodshed. As they signed treaties, others fought with the white men. In 1861 the Fort Wise Treaty pushed the tribes to southeastern Colorado, where many were executed in a surprise raid in the Sand Creek Massacre of 1864. "It will be a very hard thing to leave the country that God has gave us," he said. "Our friends are buried there, and we hate to leave these grounds." Little Raven and his family ended up on a barren reservation in Oklahoma. Meanwhile the Cheyenne Dog Soldiers who fought bitterly against white settlers went on to join the United States military and fight in both world wars and other battles.

Turn right and walk a short distance to the first gravel footpath, and turn right again to walk south back through ⓬ **Commons Park.** Keep walking south when the gravel path merges with the sidewalk again near *Common Ground*.

Walk around the hill on your right as you continue south. At the top of the grassy hill is a Sky Garden made of black granite. Often mistaken for a sundial and more public art, it is actually an installation piece put in by the landscape architects who designed the park. It points to ordinal north, south, east, and west. The view from this hilltop is pretty spectacular in any direction and can be another photo-op spot in any season. While there is no formal path or trail up the hill, winter sledders have made a scar on the north side that can serve as a trail.

Turn left on the path just past the public restrooms. Little Raven Street just ahead was named for Chief Little Raven, one of the "Peace Chiefs" who desperately tried to save this land for his people, the Arapaho, without bloodshed (see sidebar above).

Cross Little Raven Street. If it is earlier in the day, get a cup of hot coffee and a bagel at ⓭ **ink Coffee!** on your right. Walk east and head up the stairs of the Millennium Bridge, which is a funny mix of past and present with modern shiny glass and brick apartment buildings on either side and coal trains rumbling under foot on tracks below the bridge. You can see Union Station (walk 5) from up here. You have completed the loop for this walk. Be sure to take in the views once again—this is a popular place for fashion shoots and even a fashion show, so make the most of the location for your own candid shots.

Points of Interest

1. **Millennium Bridge** 16th St. between Wewatta and Little Raven Sts.
2. **Museum of Contemporary Art Denver** 1485 Delgany St., 303-298-7554, mcadenver.org
3. *Confluent People*
4. **Centennial Gardens** 1101 Little Raven St., denvergov.org
5. **Downtown Aquarium** 700 Water St., 303-561-4450, aquariumrestaurants.com
6. **The Children's Museum of Denver** 2121 Children's Museum Dr., 720-865-3585, mychildsmuseum.org
7. **Confluence Park** 15th St. between Platte and Little Raven Sts.
8. **My Brother's Bar** 2376 15th St., 303-455-9991
9. **Platte River Trail**
10. *Common Ground*
11. **Denver Skatepark** 2205 19th St., denverskatepark.com
12. **Commons Park** 15th and Little Raven Sts.
13. **ink Coffee!** 1590 Little Raven St., 720-214-111, inkcoffee.com

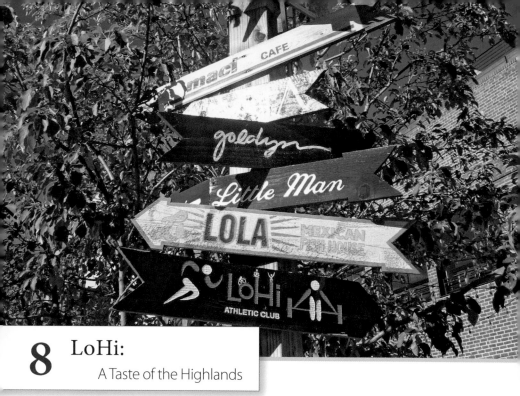

8 LoHi:
A Taste of the Highlands

BOUNDARIES: Platte St., 16th St./32nd Ave., Clay St., 33rd Ave., Osage St., Central St.
DISTANCE: 2.5 miles
DIFFICULTY: Easy
PARKING: Metered 2-hour parking is on Platte St.
PUBLIC TRANSIT: Both the 32 and 44 RTD buses stop on 15th St. at Platte St.; Denver B-cycle (denverbcycle.com) station at base of Highland Bridge on 16th and Platte St.

The neighborhood to the west of downtown is commonly called the Highlands, but it is actually a blend of historic towns and communities that were founded independently of one another and served as home for various immigrant populations over the years. The name "LoHi" is a popular nickname for Lower Highlands, but it is not an official district name. This walk takes you from historic "North Denver" beginning on Platte Street and up through what was once the town of Highland and then clips the edge of the Potter-Highlands district. Part of this tour covers what was once Acacia Cemetery in 1866, which was later moved to City Cemetery and then to Riverside Cemetery (see Walk 12). Today an old mortuary building has been turned into a home for popular restaurants, and the entire walk is sprinkled with good eats. While noshing, consider discussing the unique history of this former town whose leaders strove to make this a puritanical Eden with limits on everything from kite flying to alcohol (liquor licenses were a prohibitive $5,000 annual fee) and more in keeping with their strict moral code. I think they might approve of the ice cream parlors of today though, so go enjoy your dessert.

Walk Description

Start the walk on the northwest corner of Platte and 15th Streets. Walk north on Platte Street. There are a handful of terrific eateries and shops along this street. First up will be ❶ Sushi Sasa, next is ❷ Proto's Pizzeria, then there is the ❸ House of Commons for the tea and crumpet fix, and the strong aroma wafting out of the ❹ Savory Spice Shop might lure you inside to imagine what fabulous dishes you could create. If shopping is your thing instead of dining out, ladies walk on in to ❺ Sous le Lit and gents go to ❻ Armitage & McMillan, or the ❼ Wilderness Exchange has discounts on outdoor gear for the whole family.

Although this walk turns at 16th Street, if you were to walk north on 15th Street you would come to two other worthy drinking and dining spots: Denver Beer Co and Brider. The first is self-explanatory, and the second is a casual salad and sandwich shop with some delectable desserts and a distinguished wine list.

At 16th Street turn left toward the Highland Bridge. Before ascending the steps, you might notice another restaurant on your left, ❽ Colt & Gray, which is open for dinners featuring Colorado-sourced fare. As you walk up the steps, you can't miss (whether you want to or not) the bright red public art sculpture *National Velvet,* by artist John McEnroe, which was installed in 2008. Cross the bridge as you walk west.

Take the left fork as the bridge reaches Central Street on the other side of I-25. Cross Central Street and walk west up 16th Street. On your left will be the ❾ Masterpiece Deli, which serves a pretty perfect sandwich. Walk uphill to Boulder Street. While this walk does not turn left here, just be aware that one block away to the south are a few other places to eat: Truffle Table and Prosper Oats are a couple of my favorites.

Cross Boulder Street as you continue on 16th Street, where the old Olinger mortuary has found new life as a home to popular restaurants. To your left is ❿ Lola, with modern Mexican, and ⓫ Little Man Ice Cream, where lines stretch out into the street for their cool treats on hot summer days and nights. Special events here include outdoor movie nights and live music.

Kid Tip: Hopefully you are doing this walk on a hot afternoon so you can convince your parents to stop right here. Conveniently located right next to each other are the famed (in this neighborhood) Little Man Ice Cream and Hirshorn Park. What does Little Man Ice Cream look like, you ask? Well, it's literally a giant silver milk jug with the words LITTLE MAN ICE CREAM painted on, so it's pretty hard to miss. Hirshorn Park has a basketball court, trees for shade, and a playground!

Sort of above Little Man Ice Cream is **12 Linger** (take the *O* out of Olinger and you get . . .), a multilevel and multiethnic menu restaurant and bar. Rooftop views in summer and a killer happy hour menu make Linger quite popular. If you were to stroll up this street where 16th Street becomes 30th Avenue you would see Lulu's Furniture & Décor and, around the corner, **13 Sushi Ronin.**

Little Man Ice Cream is part of the LoHi neighborhood's busy dining scene.

As you cross 30th Avenue and veer right to walk north, note that the street grid has changed and 16th Street has divided to become both 30th Avenue going west and Tejon Street going north. On your right across the street is Hirshorn Park, a popular playground for the many families in this neighborhood and the site of the annual old-fashioned Fourth of July celebration.

Cross 31st Avenue and turn left to walk one block.

Cross Umatilla Street and turn right. This little block gives a glimpse into the common houses that were built here originally. These houses date from 1886 through 1901.

Turn left at 32nd Avenue and walk west. These next few blocks are the epicenter of real estate development in the neighborhood right now, which makes for an odd mix of sparkling new modern townhouses and FOR SALE signs on historic buildings or empty lots. On the north side of the street there is a collection of businesses, including **14 Bar Dough,** an upscale pizza place with good service and a sleek vibe.

Backstory: A Thirst for Civilization

"Water is everything," wrote the *Denver Tribune* in 1874, as the author went on to describe the land around this city as a rugged desert to be conquered. Indeed, what now seem like mere bumps in the land—Highlands, Capitol Hill—were like the mountains to the west when it came to finding a way to route enough water for early development. Smith's Ditch, a 25-mile trench, drew water from the Platte River to the dusty Capitol Hill area by 1867. Certainly the Highlands also relied on irrigated water as well, but this is also where the country's first artesian well water company was founded in 1886. According to Ruth Eloise Wiberg's book *Rediscovering Northwest Denver*, this was a time when other Denver residents had sieves on their faucets to catch the small fish that came through the new pipes with the Platte River water. That fresh artesian well water was quite welcome, and by 1886 there were over 130 artesian wells throughout Denver.

Look south as you cross Vallejo Street and you'll see the historic Asbury Church (now partially renovated into lofts), whose bell tower can be seen from downtown streets a mile away. At the corner of 32nd Avenue and Wyandot Street sits Our Merciful Savior Episcopal Church, which was built here in 1890 and has barely changed since.

Just ahead at Zuni Street and 32nd Avenue is where the neighborhood has been successfully redeveloped already with a handful of terrific restaurants. On this side of the street alone there is ⓯ Tony P's Pizzeria, ⓰ Zio Romolo's Alley Bar, and the ⓱ Wooden Spoon Café & Bakery, with pastries and sandwiches (don't miss the flaky croissants). Keep walking west on 32nd Avenue, and a few blocks farther west you will find some older establishments that reflect the Hispanic culture in the Highlands: ⓲ La Mexicana Taqueria, ⓳ Taqueria Patzcuaro, and ⓴ Panaderia Rosales.

Turn right at Clay Street and cross 32nd Avenue.

Turn right again and walk east back down 32nd Avenue. On your left will be ㉑ Park Burger—featuring seasonal fresh fruit shakes and beef and buffalo burgers—and ㉒ Spuntino, with delicious Italian small plates. The house at 2611 W. 32nd Avenue was once owned by the Coors family, of the Coors Brewery (see Walk 29).

As you approach Zuni Street again, there is a fabulous restaurant that is a must for dinner or brunch. ㉓ Duo has a seasonal menu influenced by locally grown ingredients and is on the ground floor of the historic Weir building. This is the starting point for the annual Fourth of July parade and picnic that fills the street as it winds down to Hirshorn Park.

March on down 32nd Avenue back toward downtown. At Tejon Street look south and you can see Pikes Peak when standing on the southeast corner of this intersection—on a clear day. You could easily walk right past ㉔ Williams & Graham and not realize there is a bar there, and that's kind of the point with this modern speakeasy. In the evenings, a line at the door gives this bar away, and inside it's tasty snacks and classic cocktails.

Just after Quivas Street, 32nd Avenue bends left and becomes Pecos Street, with a basketball court and small playground on one side, and just beyond that is ㉕ **Avanti Food & Beverage.** This two-story bar and "collective eatery" (sort of like indoor food trucks) attracts quite a crowd.

Walk one block to see the mission-style Capuchin order of Poor Clares and Monastery of Our Lady of Light in the former St. Patrick's Church. It is unusual to see this architectural style in Denver.

Turn right on 33rd Avenue and walk one block. At the corner of 33rd Avenue and Osage Street is ㉖ **Root Down,** a hip restaurant that highlights the building's past as a working garage in its décor and grows some of its own produce on site. Check out the great downtown views from the patio.

Turn right on Osage Street and walk one block. Turn right on 32nd Avenue and follow the sidewalk as it curves around Gateway Park on your right and you walk south along Central Street. To the east you will have a view of Coors Field baseball stadium (see Walk 5) and the downtown skyline. On your right will be ㉗ **Prost Brewing Company** for authentic German beer lovers.

If you still haven't found a place to eat, consider ㉘ **Ale House at Amato's** as Central Street meets up with 16th Street.

Turn left and cross Central Street when you reach the Highland Bridge again at 16th Street. Walk east over the bridge and back down the steps to Platte Street to end the walk.

Points of Interest

① **Sushi Sasa** 2401 15th St., 303-433-7272, sushisasa.com

② **Proto's Pizzeria** 2401 15th St., 720-855-9400, protospizza.com

③ **The House of Commons** 2401 15th St., 303-455-4832, houseofcommonstea.com

④ **Savory Spice Shop** 1537 Platte St., 720-283-2232, savoryspiceshop.com

⑤ **Sous le Lit** 1550 Platte St., 303-931-4604, souslelit.com

⑥ **Armitage & McMillan** 1550 Platte St., 303-284-6222, armitageandmcmillan.com

⑦ **Wilderness Exchange** 2401 Platte St. #100, 303-964-0708, wildernessx.com

⑧ **Colt & Gray** 1553 Platte St. #120, 303-477-1447, coltandgray.com

⑨ **Masterpiece Deli** 1575 Central St., 303-561-3354, masterpiecedeli.com

⑩ **Lola** 1575 Boulder St., 720-570-8686, loladenver.com

⑪ **Little Man Ice Cream** 2620 16th St., 303-455-3811, littlemanicecream.com

⑫ **Linger** 2030 W. 30th Ave., 303-993-3120, lingerdenver.com

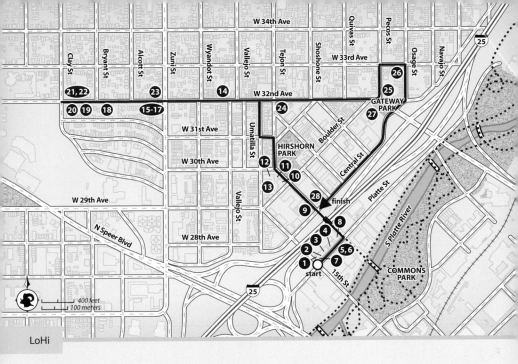

LoHi

13 **Sushi Ronin** 2930 Umatilla St., 303-955-8741, sushironindenver.com

14 **Bar Dough** 2227 W. 32nd Ave., 720-668-8506, bardoughdenver.com

15 **Tony P's Pizzeria** 2400 W. 32nd Ave., 303-477-4900, tonypspizza.com

16 **Zio Romolo's Alley Bar** 2400 W. 32nd Ave., 303-477-0395, tonypspizza.com

17 **The Wooden Spoon Café & Bakery** 2418 W. 32nd Ave., 303-999-0327, woodenspoondenver.com

18 **La Mexicana Taqueria** 2538 W. 32nd Ave., 303-433-3008, lamexicanataqueriaathighlands.com

19 **Taqueria Patzcuaro** 2616 W. 32nd Ave., 303-455-4389, patzcuaros.com

20 **Panaderia Rosales** 2636 W. 32nd Ave., 303-458-8420, rosalesbakery.com

21 **Park Burger** 2643 W. 32nd Ave., 303-862-8461, parkburger.com

22 **Spuntino** 2639 W. 32nd Ave., 303-433-0949, spuntinodenver.com

23 **Duo** 2413 W. 32nd Ave., 303-477-4141, duodenver.com

24 **Williams & Graham** 3160 Tejon St., 303-997-8886, williamsandgraham.com

25 **Avanti Food & Beverage** 3200 N. Pecos St., 720-269-4778, avantifandb.com

26 **Root Down** 1600 W. 32nd Ave., 303-993-4200, rootdowndenver.com

27 **Prost Brewing Company** 2540 19th St., 303-729-1175, prostbrewing.com

28 **Ale House at Amato's** 2501 16th St., 303-433-9734, alehousedenver.com

9 Highlands Square:
It's Hip to be Square

Above: *Highlands Square is home to many boutiques and restaurants.*   *photo courtesy of Visit Denver*

BOUNDARIES: Grove St., Speer Blvd., 32nd Ave. Perry St.
DISTANCE: 0.5 mile to 1 mile
DIFFICULTY: Easy
PARKING: Free 2-hour parking on streets
PUBLIC TRANSIT: RTD 32 bus stops at Highland Park.

Some might say that Highlands Square is the heart of the Highlands neighborhood, with its cluster of locally owned shops and restaurants within easy walking distances to blocks and blocks of charming historic homes. It should be noted though that there is no actual square, but rather a few consecutive blocks with businesses shoulder-to-shoulder, which makes it an ideal place for an afternoon or evening stroll. Highlands Square is host to a few annual events, which can help you plan the best time for a walk. In June there is the annual street fair—which has been going on for more than 25 years—as well as a sidewalk sale; in every season except winter on the third Thursday of each month there is a sort of wandering happy hour along the avenue; Halloween brings trick or treating with costumed children going door to door in daylight; and during the holidays there are horse-drawn carriage rides.

Walk Description

Begin this walk on the western edge of Highland Park at Grove Street. Back across the park is
❶ **Woodbury Library.** The library is named for Brigadier General Roger W. Woodbury, who came to Denver in 1866 as a Civil War Veteran and became a businessman, politician, and first president of the Denver Chamber of Commerce. Woodbury was a founder of the public library and persuaded Andrew Carnegie to make a large donation. This library is the only reminder of Woodbury's Denver life, since his own palatial home in the neighborhood was razed in the 1950s. The library was designed by architect J. J. B. Benedict (see Walk 25).

> **Kid Tip:** As you walk through the park, there is a playground just across from the Bosler House, so you (and your siblings or friends) can play there for a bit during the walk! There are little slides for very young kids, and a climbing area for bigger kids.

Cross Grove Street. On the corner behind the hedges is the landmark-designated Bosler House, built in 1891, and down the street is what was once the Tilden Health School and Sanitarium, likely serving tuberculosis patients as well as others (Dr. John H. Tilden is considered one of the pioneers of natural medicine in the United States). Tuberculosis brought many people in search of a cure for the fatal illness to Denver as they sought relief in the thin, dry, clean air. It has even been said that tuberculosis brought more people to settle in the Mile High City than the possibility of mining riches did. Research shows that one-third of Colorado residents in 1900 had the disease. Being situated above the pollution of Denver's downtown made Highlands a natural setting for

Historical buildings are home to modern businesses.

sanitariums where patients could rest and recuperate—in both semipermanent tent camps and hospitals. The city's largest tubercular home was a complex of 25 buildings just east of Federal Boulevard on 32nd Avenue until the early 1930s, when it was closed. Some of those who came here seeking a cure became prominent citizens, such as popular Mayor Robert Speer. All of the structures on this block at one time served as some sort of health-care facility, and some have now been converted to condominiums.

Cross Fairview Place and walk west on Grove Street one block.

Cross Grove Street again to reach the crosswalk at Green Court and Speer Boulevard.

Cross Speer Boulevard and begin walking west on 32nd Avenue. At Irving Street will be ❷ **The Denver Bread Company,** where you must stop in for at least a sample bite of their heavenly bread or the Victory + Love cookies they sell. Craving spice instead? Catty-corner is a second location of Tacos Tequila Whiskey (see Walk 17), which is also called Pinche Tacos.

Cross Irving Street and continue walking on 32nd Avenue. Though a continuous block, this next stretch past small Victorian-era homes feels like at least two blocks. At Julian Street you begin to enter the business district of Highlands Square, with Three Dogs Tavern on the left side of the street. If you like a game of pool with your beer, this is the neighborhood spot for you.

After you cross Julian Street and continue west on 32nd Avenue, you will see ❸ **Happy Bakeshop** and ❹ **West Side Books** on the south side of the street. I love the mini cupcakes at Happy Bakeshop, and West Side Books offers an intriguing mix of used, new, and unusual books. It's one shop and eatery after another for the next two blocks! One place I like to go for girly gifts is ❺ **Starlet;** next you can stop for brunch or dinner at ❻ **Trattoria Stella** for hearty and creative Italian cuisine. I'm not listing every place to shop or eat, just the ones I'm partial to, but enjoy exploring to find your favorites.

Kid Tip: If you have a sweet tooth, this stop is for you! On 32nd Avenue, just off Lowell, is ❼ **Sweet Cow Ice Cream!** My friends and I often walk here after school, and we all think it's great. So you can stop in here for a quick break during your walk! My recommendation? A cookies and cream shake with whipped cream! For sure ask your parents to stop here.

As you cross Lowell Boulevard, take notice of ❽ **St. Kilian's Cheese Shop** to your right, where you can ask for a sample of the unique cheeses before buying. St. Kilian's is where I like to stop in for the perfect picnic or hiking—or walking!—snacks. In the opposite direction is ❾ **Sushi Hai,** quite the date night staple for this neighborhood. As you keep walking, on your left on 32nd Avenue is ❿ **The Perfect Petal** for flowers, gifts, and cards. El Camino Community Tavern is poplar for margaritas and tacos—think ladies' night, or happy hour. Across the street is ⓫ **Strut**

Backstory: Highlands History

As Denver and the Highlands neighborhoods were being settled in the 1800s, immigrant populations were carving out their own niches. The Highlands area attracted working-class German, English, Irish, and Italian immigrants who moved to North Denver and established their own churches, shops, and restaurants specializing in their own cultural heritage. The Italians were probably the most deeply established; parts of the Highlands were known as Little Italy for many years, and there were Italian language newspapers and a bank. As time went on, groups would complain of being pushed out by the next larger one, and the last were the Italians who were seemingly replaced by Latinos. Today that population is being edged out by gentrification, though there are still vestiges of those former cultures—particularly Italian and Latino—sprinkled throughout the Highlands.

for fashionable shoes and ⑫ **Dragonfly** with stylish clothes to coordinate with those new shoes. ⑬ **Mead Street Station** is another neighborhood staple with live music and dependably good burgers and salads.

At the corner of Meade Street you'll see ⑭ **Kismet**—a gem of a place for women's accessories—and Wordshop tucked in behind it, for those still using stationery and stamps (like me!). You don't just have to walk by the historic houses on this tour—you can go right inside. Stop in at Nostalgic Homes in the 1890 house at 3737 32nd Avenue to see inside a gorgeous historic home and maybe see what's for sale nearby too.

Specialty shops such as St. Kilian's are part of Highlands Square.

Keep walking west on 32nd Avenue. At Osceola is the Highlands United Methodist Church, which is often host to classes for youth and other activities.

Just before Perry Street is ⑮ **Blue Pan Pizza**—delish! It's a huge dine-in space, but so good!

The walk can end here and you can loop back to the starting point—after stopping to shop and eat, of course—or you can walk south down Perry Street (or any of the streets you have just crossed) about one mile to 25th Street, then west to Tennyson Street and to Sloan's Lake Park. The next chapter provides detail on a walk around Sloan's Lake Park (Walk 10).

Highlands Square

Points of Interest

1. **Woodbury Library** 3265 Federal Blvd., denverlibrary.org
2. **The Denver Bread Company** 3200 Irving St., 303-455-7194, thedenverbreadcompany.com
3. **Happy Bakeshop** 3434 W. 32nd Ave., 303-477-3556, happybakeshopcolorado.com
4. **West Side Books** 3434 W. 32nd Ave., 303-480-0220, westsidebooks.com
5. **Starlet** 3450 W. 32nd Ave., 303-433-7827, www.shopstarlet.com
6. **Trattoria Stella** 3470 W. 32nd Ave., 303-458-1128, trattoriastella.squarespace.com
7. **Sweet Cow Ice Cream** 3475 W. 32nd Ave., 303-477-3269, sweetcowicecream.com
8. **St. Kilian's Cheese Shop** 3211 Lowell Blvd., 303-477-0374, stkilianscheeseshop.com
9. **Sushi Hai** 3600 W. 32nd Ave., 720-855-0888, sushihai.com
10. **The Perfect Petal** 3600 W. 32nd Ave., 303-480-0966, theperfectpetal.com
11. **Strut** 3611 W. 32nd Ave., 303-477-3361, strutdenver.com
12. **Dragonfly** 3615 W. 32nd Ave., 303-433-6331, facebook.com/DragonflyApparel
13. **Mead St. Station** 3625 W. 32nd Ave., 303-433-2138, meadststation.com
14. **Kismet** 3640 W. 32nd Ave., 303-477-3378, kismetaccessories.com
15. **Blue Pan Pizza** 3930 W. 32nd Ave., 720-456-7666, bluepandenver.com

10 Sloan's Lake Park:
Pick Your View

Above: *Sloan's Lake Park hosts the annual Colorado Dragon Boat Festival.*
photographed by Dawn Jacoby/Colorado Dragon Boat Festival

BOUNDARIES: Sheridan Blvd., 26th Ave., 17th Ave., Stuart St./20th Ave./Lakeshore Dr.
DISTANCE: 3 miles
DIFFICULTY: Easy
PARKING: Free parking is available in lots around the outskirts of the park.
PUBLIC TRANSIT: The 28 RTD Bus runs along 26th Ave.

It has jokingly been called Sloan's Leak for the amusing way this large urban lake was discovered. In 1861 farmer Thomas Sloan was digging a well for desperately needed water on these dry plains, only to check on it later and find a flood in his fields. By the time it was done gushing, and Denver citizens and Native Americans alike had come out on horseback to watch it, Farmer Sloan had a 200-acre lake where his crops were supposed to be. It quickly became a popular recreation spot and remains so today as Denver's second-largest park. The Rocky Mountain vista to the west offers gorgeous views, particularly at sunset, and to the east looking over the tree canopies of the Highlands neighborhood is the downtown Denver skyline. Sloan's Lake itself is ringed by a sidewalk where you see parents pushing their jogging strollers, cyclists zipping past, and pedestrians ambling by; out on the water look for boaters in canoes, kayaks, and sailboats, all with various wildlife splashing around. The park is host to the annual Colorado Dragon Boat Festival, a celebration of Asian cultures and an elaborately decorated boat race across the lake.

Note: As in other park walks, footpaths do cross roads within the park. Please use caution when off the designated footpath. Also keep in mind that there is very little shade along this walk.

Walk Description

Begin this walk from the north side parking lot at 26th Avenue and Tennyson Street by the tennis courts. Walk toward the playground and follow the concrete sidewalk path to the left as it slopes downhill. Continue downhill toward the lake as the concrete path becomes black asphalt.

Kid Tip: This is the first of two playgrounds on this walk! Almost as soon as you start this walk, there is a first playground, smaller than the second, but still a good stop. The second, larger playground is about halfway through, a good spot to stop, rest for a minute, and play!

Cautiously cross Byron Place near 24th Avenue, as this is a regular street with car traffic.

Walk to the concrete path that circumvents the lake and turn right. Keep in mind that this wide path is shared by pedestrians and cyclists. This is your first view of the snow-capped Rocky Mountains to the west. A reconstructed historic jetty with pavilion is on the north side of the lake, with 60 slips for rental boats, just steps from the historic bathhouse and restrooms.

To your right, back across Byron Place, you will notice the hodgepodge of architectural vintages and styles in the houses of this neighborhood. There are trilevel moderns next door to Spanish-style villas and everything in between.

As you approach Sheridan Boulevard, walking west, take note of a sign on your right near a dock. The sign has one historical photograph of boaters in the lake's early days, as well as detailed information on the water quality. Despite the fact that the lake is open to fishing, boating, and even waterskiing, it is polluted. The lake is stocked with carp, channel catfish, rainbow trout, and more. Permits are required for boating and licenses for fishing, which is only allowed from the shore. Sloan's Lake does partially freeze over in winter, but it is not solid enough for people to walk on it.

Stay on the path as it curves to the left and becomes parallel with Sheridan Boulevard. Just across this busy street is the town of Edgewater, founded in 1861 and part of Jefferson County.

As the Highlands neighborhood has become increasingly popular and pricey, Edgewater has gained new appeal with its proximity to the amenities of Highlands and more affordable real estate. The place with the most history is the ❶ **Edgewater Inn,** just a block off Sheridan Boulevard and 25th Avenue (Byron Place becomes 25th Avenue after crossing Sheridan Boulevard), where people come for pizza and *schooners* of beer in a family-friendly atmosphere. In the newer strip malls along Sheridan Boulevard you'll find ❷ **Rupert's at the Edge** for a hearty breakfast and ❸ **GB Fish and Chips,** where the GB stands for Get Battered and not Great Britain, despite the English food menu.

This stretch of the walk offers the best view of the city's downtown skyline when you look to the east back over Sloan's Lake. It was from this vantage point that dreams of making the lake a play land were hatched—over and over again.

Artist Kristine Smock's sculpture *The Denver* honors a steamship that once crossed Sloan's Lake.

Once Thomas Sloan had secured the rights to all of the land that the lake was now on, he developed a prosperous icehouse on the lakeshore. In 1872 he sold and moved away. Although the lake had become a fashionable place for swimming, boating, and ice-skating, plans to make it a more formal park kept falling through. The first of a handful of resorts and amusement parks here was Sloan's Lake Resort, which opened in 1890, complete with sailboats, rental boats, and a rigged-up barge called the *City of Denver.* In 1891, all of the resort's buildings were burned to the ground. But this just opened the door for someone else's dream, and on this side of the lake the Manhattan Beach Company opened an even grander amusement park later in 1891. With formal gardens, zoo animals, a new sandy beach, a large auditorium, and other attractions, Manhattan Beach was a success. Then in 1908, it too burned up. Next up was Luna Park in 1909, and a main attraction was the *Frolic,* a three-deck side-wheeler boat. Competition with the other amusement parks

Backstory: Goose on the Loose

Enjoying that almost year-round sunshine we get here in Denver? You're not the only one. Turns out the Mile High City's climate is mild enough to be considered south for migrating Canadian geese. Certainly not all of the thousands of geese populating Denver parks are seasonal visitors; some are actually residents. Either way, these animals are rather messy and can leave the walkways and lawns of parks an unpleasant mess with their droppings.

Try to time your walk with the migration of the geese for the cleanest walk season. In late summer and early fall, the goose population is at its lowest—plus, the temperatures are mild and the leaves are changing pretty colors. It's likely that goose sightings and droppings will be at a minimum during this time of year. Their numbers explode in winter, and unfortunately that means when the flowers are in bloom and the warmth of summer is coming on, the geese are molting and their population is at its most dense in the parks.

---

in Highlands hastened Luna Park's demise, and the city bought up the land to eventually turn it into the park it is today.

Cross the footbridge as the path again curves left and you will be walking east, parallel to 17th Avenue. You will notice a small fort-style building on the right as the path returns to concrete. This was built in 1923 as the Denver Municipal Trap Club, and members came here to practice their shooting skills with pigeons as targets. After noise complaints forced them to close, the Sloan's Lake Boxing Club took over the space. On the other side of this building is a memorial for the ❹ USS *Grayling*, which was lost with a full submarine crew in 1943 during World War II.

In fall the cottonwood trees, maple trees, and willow trees make this part of the walk very colorful as the leaves go from green to sunshine yellow, orange, and gold. Also, early fall is the best time to walk around this or any other park because the city's enormous Canadian geese population is at its lowest, so the paths are very clean.

As you approach the next playground area, be sure to stop and read the sign with lots of historical photographs of the park and detailed information about the lake use.

Even after the amusement parks were long gone, into the 1940s people came here for boat races regularly. To see the modern dragon boat races, check cdbf.org for the current festival dates.

The path curves left again as you near West Lakeshore Drive and cross a footbridge. You are now walking north. To your right is Lake Middle School, which opened in 1926 as a junior high school. Architects Merrill and Burnham Hoyt, best known for designing the Red Rocks

Amphitheatre (see Walk 27), designed the school. It is a combination of design elements, to be sure, with Tudor arches and parapets, elaborate brickwork, and towers.

The public art **5** *The Denver,* by artist Kristine Smock, is a tribute to the steamship that once drew thousands of visitors to Sloan's Lake.

This portion is historically called Cooper Lake, a man-made creation formed when a canal was dug from the south side of Sloan's Lake to a hotel a mile away. The canal was wide enough for a small steamship launch and caused Sloan's Lake to empty into the low area to the east. This gives the combined lakes an hourglass shape from above. The combined lakes are 177 acres (portions of the original Sloan's Lake were filled in years ago, shrinking it from its 200 acres).

The rest of this walk in any season offers the most incredible views of the Rocky Mountains, really giving you a sense of the vast length of the 140-mile range visible from the Mile High City. It's funny that Sloan's Lake feels like a relatively low flat spot, and the view is so great. There are benches here and there where you can sit and gaze out at the water and mountains, with the skyline at your back.

The island between Sloan's and Cooper Lakes is a bird sanctuary and off-limits to humans.

The path curves to the left again as you almost complete the loop.

Turn right to cross Byron Place and walk up the hill back to the playground and parking lot. This walk can be combined with Walk 9 by walking east on 26th Street to Perry Street, then north on Perry Street to 32nd Avenue. Or it can be combined with Walk 11 by walking 1 mile on Tennyson Street to 38th Avenue.

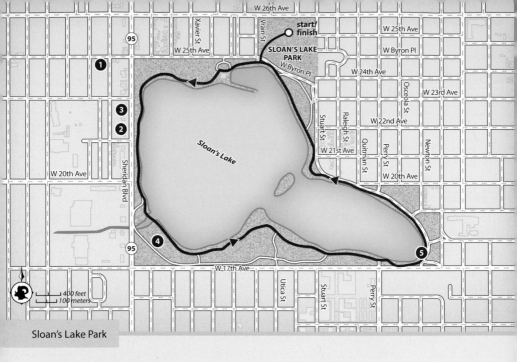

Points of Interest

1. **Edgewater Inn** 5302 W. 25th Ave., 303-237-3524, edgewaterinn.net

2. **Rupert's at the Edge** 2045 Sheridan Blvd., 720-328-5806, eatatruperts.com

3. **GB Fish and Chips** 2175 Sheridan Blvd., 303-232-2138, gbfishandchips.com

4. **USS *Grayling*** Sloan's Lake Park

5. ***The Denver*** Sloan's Lake Park

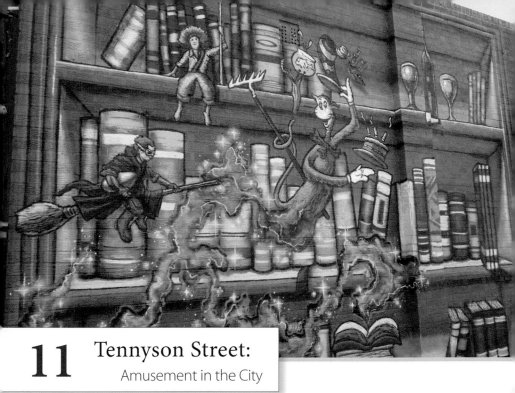

11 Tennyson Street:
Amusement in the City

BOUNDARIES: 38th Ave., Tennyson St., 46th Ave., Sheridan Blvd.
DISTANCE: 2.5 miles
DIFFICULTY: Easy
PARKING: 2-hour free parking is available on Tennyson St.
PUBLIC TRANSIT: RTD 38 bus runs along 38th Ave.

The greater Highlands neighborhood (what is collectively called the Highlands today is actually many small historic neighborhoods) was once home to three amusement parks that all competed for customers beginning in the late 1800s. Into the 1990s, there were still two of these historic amusement parks standing and in use, and now just one remains, which you will see on this walk. Perhaps it was the combination of open land, the strict moral codes of the neighborhood that forbid alcohol sales for many years, and a desire to get out of the hectic downtown for a little clean fun nearby that made Highlands a natural place to develop gardens, add some animals, and throw in a few thrill rides. Elitch Gardens was the best-known amusement park—in Denver and beyond—and this walk begins on the site of the park's remains that are now surrounded by urban infill housing. For several blocks, Tennyson Street is a thriving business district filled with shops, restaurants, and art galleries. As the walk comes to an end after a stroll through Berkeley Park, you will have a chance to experience living history at Lakeside Amusement Park, the city's last historic amusement park still in operation since its opening in 1908.

Walk Description

Start your walk under the old Elitch's Pavilion at the corner of 38th Avenue and Tennyson Street. This used to be where the park's carousel twirled visitors around and around; it's now used for various community events. Look out the sides of the pavilion to see the historic theatre, the only remaining original building from the park. Elitch Gardens was opened in 1890 when John and Mary Elitch transformed an apple orchard and garden into a family-friendly resort with zoo animals, a professional theatre, vaudeville acts, and rides. The park changed with the times—going from an emphasis on theatre to hosting large dances in the Trocadero building, and then adding roller coasters and thrill rides. In 1994, Elitch's was "relocated" to the Central Platte Valley, and this 28-acre site was transformed into Highlands Garden Village, a "New Urbanism" layout of 300 housing units and businesses.

Cross 38th Avenue to begin walking north up Tennyson Street. This section of Highlands is actually called Berkeley, just like the park you will come to near the end of the walk. As you walk along Tennyson Street you will see yoga studios, hair salons, an old-style barbershop, bookstores, art galleries, coffee shops, boutiques, bars, restaurants, and a playground. Oh, and a cat café. A big event takes place here every Halloween when five blocks of Tennyson Street are filled with costumed youngsters trick-or-treating at the local businesses in the middle of the day. The first Friday of the month is occasion for a "culture walk" among the businesses.

Tennyson Street is evolving, with old businesses—and even sometimes the buildings they were in for generations—disappearing and new startups in their place. Chances are that you'll make some discoveries not mentioned here as the change continues.

Just after crossing 39th Avenue on your left is ❶ **Vital Root,** a vegetarian restaurant with the emphasis on vegetables. Everything served is like a work of vegetable art.

Across the street is ❷ **Hops & Pie,** where pizza toppings include bacon, pulled pork, and mashed potatoes, as well as vegan options. Go early and expect to wait because it's popular.

Back on the west side of the street is the ❸ **Denver Cat Company.** You know your city has reached ultimate hipsterness when you get a cat café. If you can't or don't have a feline at home, here you can cuddle and relax with a cup of coffee, a book, and a kitty. There is a cover charge to come in and pet the cats or paint portraits of them during a sipping and painting event.

On the other side of the street you will find ❹ **Block & Larder.** Bring your appetite and maybe not the kids for dishes like cassoulet or trying the "eclectic whiskey" and bourbon selection.

Ladies, take a minute to step into Lady Jones, a boutique where you can find that next great little black dress or some stylish jeans.

A holdout from the Tennyson Street of yore is Kyle's Kitchen next door. It's a comfy and simple spot for a cup of coffee—love sitting at the "bar"—or a full meal. I'm a biscuits-and-gravy kind of gal, and this is a no frills place for just that kind of stick-to-your-ribs meal.

A few doors down is ❺ **Allegro Coffee,** not your old funky college coffee shop. In what was formerly a neighborhood hardware store is a chic place for staying caffeinated and plugged in, maybe holding a business meeting over a locally made pastry.

You've since passed a couple of bars on the other side of the street. At ❻ **West End Tap House** you can sample many a Colorado beer and have a bite to eat.

The blocks don't quite match as you cross the street, but keep going north on Tennyson Street.

Kid Tip: "The fight is never about grapes or lettuce. It is always about people." This quote is written on the side of Cesar E. Chavez Park, and I'll leave it to you to imagine or figure out what it means and the connection to the park. The park is a great place to stop on your walk and play—some open field and a jungle gym that's pretty fun as well. Keep in mind, this isn't the only park and playground on this walk.

With the park on your left, across the street to your right is Inspyre Boutique, a women's boutique that has high fashion and low prices—a better combination than matching shoes and purse!

After walking past Cesar E. Chavez Park, the business district continues with more bars, restaurants, and shops. In a former dance school you will find the ❼ **Denver Biscuit Company, Fat Sully's Pizza,** and **Atomic Cowboy.** This is a strange concept, but this is not their only Denver location, where, depending on the time of day, you can get a Southern-style biscuit breakfast, a hot slice, or a cold adult beverage. This too is a kid-friendly place, and I see families in here whenever I go.

Men, I didn't forget you. There's a boutique for your clothing needs too. ❽ **Berkeley Supply** has T-shirts, jeans, boots, and more for the urban guy, with an emphasis on American made.

In fact, the whole family can shop on this street. ❾ **Real Baby** has that perfect onesie, book, toy, wrap, everything you need for the bambino in your life.

Now it's time to cross the street to ❿ **BookBar,** a wine bar and bookstore with a book-themed menu, a summer patio, a cozy fireside reading room, and even BookBed upstairs, a swanky vacation rental for the traveling author or their adoring readership.

Just before 44th Avenue on the right is ⑪ **Swing Thai,** with a lovely hidden patio out back. At the corner of 44th Avenue and Tennyson Street is one of the neighborhood's more popular restaurants, ⑫ **Parisi Italian Market & Deli.** With a menu of pizza, pasta, and gelato, what's not to like?

Along 44th Avenue to the east is the Oriental Theater, a vintage movie theatre from the 1920s that is now a music venue. For a simple—and affordable—dinner, try Empanda Express Grill, which is arguably the best place in the city for these savory Venezuelan meal pockets.

Just around the corner back on Tennyson Street is Tenn Street Coffee & Books, which has books for sale and regular live music performances. Next you will see the Tennyson Studios, a collection of art galleries open during First Friday, and other times as well, to show off local budding artists.

Continue walking north on Tennyson Street as the next two blocks become mostly residential, with two notable exceptions: ⑬ **MAS KAOS Pizzeria + Taqueria** and ⑭ **Local 46.** Pizza *and* tacos, in the same place! Local 46 is a wonderful neighborhood bar that has perfectly mixed the old vibe with new style, and the best time to be here is in the spring and summer when you can sit outside, play a little cornhole, and relax in their biergarten.

Turn left on 46th Avenue after you cross the street to Berkeley Park and walk west on the paved path that is parallel to the park. Berkeley Park has tennis courts, a playground, a recreation center, and 43-acre Berkeley Lake. You can rent canoes, kayaks, and paddleboats at the lake in summer (wheelfunrentals.com).

On your right is the Smiley Branch Library, which was built with funds from the Carnegie Library Corporation at the turn of the century. Smiley was completed in 1918 and is one of only a handful of the Carnegie-funded libraries still open as a library in Denver.

The footpath will end as you get to the Scheitler Recreation Center parking lot. You can continue walking west on the grass to Sheridan Boulevard. Dog lovers may note that there is a designated dog park off to the right, next to I-70 on the park's north flank.

Cross Sheridan Boulevard to ⑮ **Lakeside Amusement Park.** Even when the park is closed, you can peer in the gates and get a glimpse of the retro rides inside. Opened in 1908, Lakeside's light tower, "Tower of Jewels," was the tallest structure in the state—quite a brilliant sight on the wide-open prairie here. The carousel is original, and the miniature trains are from the 1904 St. Louis World's Fair. While there are some newer rides, the older ones with the Art Deco fixtures and neon are still so fun. The 1940s wooden Cyclone Coaster is a designated landmark. Open during summer only, the amusement park takes up half of what is the small town of Lakeside for several blocks.

Kid Tip: At Lakeside's Kiddie Playland, try to get the Denver Broncos car on the spinning ride.

Turn around and walk back the way you came to finish the loop. This walk can be combined with Walk 10 by walking 1 mile south on Tennyson Street to 26th Street.

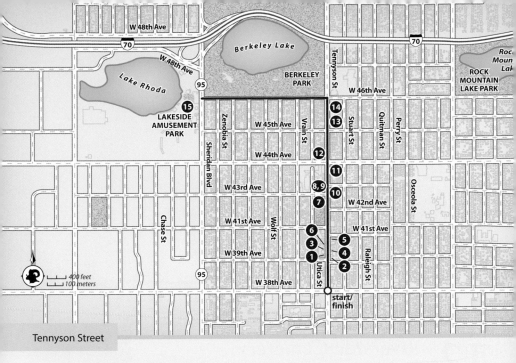

Tennyson Street

Points of Interest

1. **Vital Root** 3915 Tennyson St., 303-474-4131, vitalrootdenver.com
2. **Hops & Pie** 3920 Tennyson St., 303-477-7000, hopsandpie.com
3. **Denver Cat Company** 3929 Tennyson St., 303-433-3422, denvercatco.com
4. **Block & Larder** 4000 Tennyson St. #101, 303-433-4063, blockandlarder.com
5. **Allegro Coffee** 4040 Tennyson St., 720-630-8157, allegrocoffee.com
6. **West End Tap House** 3945 Tennyson St., 303-433-4759, westendtaphouse.com
7. **Denver Biscuit Co, Fat Sully's, Atomic Cowboy** 4275 Tennyson St., 303-377-7900, denbisco.com; 303-393-1515, fatsullys.com; and atomiccowboy.net
8. **Berkeley Supply** 4309 Tennyson St., 720-445-6818, berkeleysupply.com
9. **Real Baby** 4315 Tennyson St., 303-477-2229, realbabyinc.com
10. **BookBar** 4280 Tennyson St., 303-284-0194, bookbardenver.com
11. **Swing Thai** 4370 Tennyson St., 303-477-1994, swingthai.com
12. **Parisi Italian Market & Deli** 4401 Tennyson St., 303-561-0234, parisidenver.com
13. **MAS KAOS Pizzeria + Taqueria** 4526 Tennyson St., 720-638-2100, maskaosdenver.com
14. **Local 46** 4586 Tennyson St., 720-524-3792, local46bar.com
15. **Lakeside Amusement Park** 4601 Sheridan Blvd., 303-477-1621, lakesideamusementpark.com

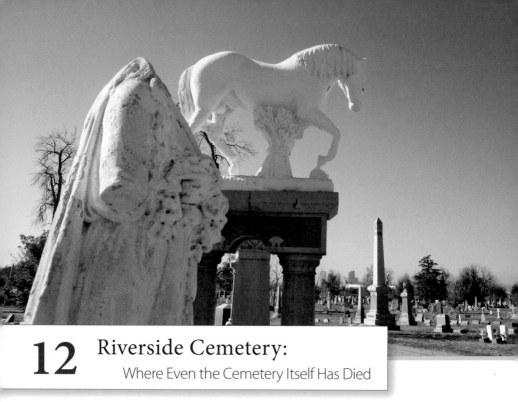

12 Riverside Cemetery:
Where Even the Cemetery Itself Has Died

Above: Many of the headstones and statues in Riverside Cemetery have fallen into disrepair.

BOUNDARIES: Brighton Blvd., York St., South Platte River
DISTANCE: 1.5 miles
DIFFICULTY: Easy
PARKING: Free parking is available inside the cemetery.
PUBLIC TRANSIT: RTD 48 bus makes stops on Brighton Blvd.

Riverside Cemetery is Denver's oldest cemetery, though not its first. Cemeteries in the Cheesman Park and Highlands neighborhoods were closed, and the bodies of those interred were moved to Riverside shortly after it opened in 1876. At the time it was a welcome alternative to the neglected and damaged cemeteries in the city, but now Riverside itself is dying. The short version is this: Riverside has not been watered since 2003. It's one irony on top of another: a place devoted to the dead was designed to attract the living with its parklike setting of shade trees and flower beds next to a river, but research in the 1980s determined the cemetery did not actually have water rights to the nearby river and the tap was shut off for this 77-acre cemetery. This designated national historic district is located just two miles from downtown and partially in the industrial zone of Commerce City. Some of Denver's earliest pioneers and most notable citizens who shaped the city and state lie here, as well as servicemen from the Civil War through the Gulf War, and various clusters of headstones devoted to different religious and ethnic groups are seen here. Rocky Mountain views to the west are visible from just about anywhere in the cemetery, and from other vantage points you will see the city's skyline as you wander amongst the eerie and beautiful historic headstones.

Note: All of the gravel pathways on this walk are roads, and cars do have access at all times too. Riverside Cemetery is open daily, 8 a.m.–5 p.m.

Walk Description

Begin the walk in front of the office, which is to the right of the gated entrance. (At the time of this writing, the Public Utilities Commission was trying to force the closure of Riverside's historic entrance. Presumably there will be signs installed directing visitors to a new entrance if this effort was successful.) Volunteers generally staff the office on Tuesdays and Thursdays and the first Wednesday of every month. On the left side of the building is a small chapel with wooden pews and a stained glass window, and in the office are the original handwritten internment ledgers and maps. No matter where you are in the cemetery, the coal trains rumbling by and blowing their whistles are audible, but as you get deeper into the cemetery the sounds and industrial fumes seem to fade away.

The office and entrance area are part of the 12% of Riverside that actually lies within the Denver County limits, while the rest of the cemetery is part of Adams County.

According to the Friends of Historic Riverside Cemetery, a nonprofit group of volunteers trying to help preserve the cemetery, of the 67,000 people buried at Riverside only about half have grave markers. Riverside was dedicated as a National Historic District in 1992.

Walk around the left of the flagpole area while staying on the gravel footpath. You'll see a small green marker with a white 36 painted on it to your left. Continue to follow the path as it curves left past green marker 35.

At the 19 marker, you will see the blue and white St. Michael's Plot, erected in 1918. According to Annette L. Student in her excellent book, *Denver's Riverside Cemetery: Where History Lies,* this plot is used for members of the Holy Transfiguration of Christ Orthodox Cathedral, which is located in nearby Globeville and was founded by Russian and Serbian immigrants.

Turn right and walk north so that St. Michael's Plot is on your left.

Veer right again to walk between section 16 on the left and 15 on the right. (Note that St. Michael's Plot was in the little 19 section and adjacent to the little 15 section, both of which have larger sections with the same number on the east side of this path.)

Make a hard left at the six-point intersection. To your right is a 2003 Colorado Confederate Veterans Memorial with flagpole.

Turn left again to walk parallel to the cemetery's three mausoleums in what is called "the bottoms" of Riverside. Annette Student reports in her book that the first mausoleum is actually empty. Businessman Hartsville F. Jones was never buried in this mausoleum. Next up is the underground mausoleum of Martha T. Evans and seven other family members. Although locked wrought iron gates secure the tomb, the wooden doors that cover the stairs to the underground chamber are no longer in place, and you can feel the cool air from below on the hottest day. It's a creepy spot. Martha T. Evans (no relation to John Evans and family, who will be mentioned later on the tour) moved to Denver in 1882 with her children and worked as treasurer of a candy company, writes Student. The third mausoleum is for Ovando James Hollister, who came to Colorado to farm in the 1850s, then joined the Colorado Infantry during the Civil War, and later became an editor of the *Rocky Mountain News*.

Turn around and walk north back toward the flagpole. On your left is private cemetery property, but also the history of the water issues at Riverside. The South Platte River lies to the west and was the original water source for the cemetery's thousands of trees. After losing their free water access rights, Fairmount Cemetery Company, the owners of Riverside since 1900, fought the decision all the way to the Colorado Supreme Court and lost. In 2003 Fairmount could no longer afford to pay for watering Riverside, and it has been dry ever since. The small reservoir below is home to various birds and wildlife throughout the year. Walking across this crunchy, desiccated ground does give one the sense of what Colorado's pioneers faced when they first came to these arid plains and tried to farm and build.

Turn right and walk up the small hill with the first mausoleum on your right.

At the six-point intersection again, turn left to walk on the path in front of the stone house. This is the only other office building at the cemetery, but it is not open to the public.

As you continue walking north, section 13 on your left has three notable markers. The first is a large granite marker with the name EVANS for Evan E. Evans and his wife, Annie Cecilia Evans. Mr. Evans was the son of John Evans, whose own gray granite memorial is in the same section just ahead. The elder Mr. Evans was appointed by Abraham Lincoln to be the second territorial governor of Colorado from 1862 to 1865, and Mount Evans just west of Denver is named after him. His wife, Margaret Evans, is buried next to him, according to Student's book. (See Walk 2 for information on the Byers-Evans House owned by William Evans.) Nearby is the headstone for Samuel Hitt Elbert, who also served as a governor of the Territory of Colorado. Although you may not be able to see them from this spot, there are two impressive mountain peaks named after these men—Mount Evan and Mount Elbert—in Colorado's Rocky Mountains.

Back here in the cemetery, you may be wondering if that man on a grave marker has a mountain named after him. Alas, no, he does not. That is a bronze statue replica of Colonel James Archer atop the 10-foot-high granite grave marker. He is best known for creating the Denver Gas Works, which brought gas lighting to streetlights and people's homes in the late 1870s.

Turn right to walk east, with section 4 on your left and section 5 on the right. About half-way down section 4 is a large boulder marker for Katrina Murat, the third white woman to live in Denver, writes Student, and known as the "Mother of Colorado" for making the first US flag (from her own clothes, no less!) to fly over Denver in 1859. Her husband, Count Henri Murat, has a flat marker in front of hers, and if you read more history on this couple you'll see why that is a fitting arrangement.

At the next intersection you do not even need to turn to see a white horse on top of a memorial. According to Student, the sandstone horse "is the only one of its kind in a U.S. cemetery." Her research found that the family of Addison Baker had the statue made for his grave because of his love of horses. He is remembered for delivering fresh water in barrels to Denver residents in 1860 from a freshwater spring on his property in West Denver.

Lester Drake's Cabin

Turn left and walk to Lester Drake's Cabin, perhaps the most unique headstone here—or anywhere. Research by the Friends of Historic Riverside Cemetery found that Lester Drake was a gold miner in Black Hawk, Colorado, and this limestone monument is a replica of his mining cabin. The detail in the front of the cabin includes mining tools.

Turn right into the circular section 7.

Turn left almost immediately and walk south. Just behind a large marker with the name GIBSON is a smaller monument for Augusta Tabor (she has two markers here: the smaller one chosen by her, the other a

Some of Denver's most prominent early residents are buried at Riverside Cemetery.

dedication), which describes her as the "epitome of a pioneer." Tabor came to Colorado with her husband, Horace Tabor, who went on to make a fortune in Leadville's Matchless Mine and then divorced Augusta after he fell in love with a woman who came to be known as "Baby Doe."

Walk right as the circle turns. On the left you will see the gray draped urn marking the Zang burial plots. Philip Zang came from Germany in the 1860s and established the Zang Brewery, which during its peak was the largest brewery between San Francisco and Saint Louis.

Walk right around the circle and to your left is the gray granite obelisk for Miguel Antonio Otero, whom Student describes as the "first native New Mexican elected as a delegate to the U.S. Congress" in 1855. For reasons not given, Otero did not want to be buried in New Mexico. Just to the right of Otero's marker—and much closer to the ground—is the headstone for Roger Woodbury, for whom the Woodbury Branch Library in the Highlands neighborhood is named (see Walk 9).

Take the first left out of the circle and walk east.

Take the left fork in the path and walk with section 5 on your left and section 4 on your right.

Turn right to walk north and again past Col. Archer. The plot on the left with the white marble cross is the only section of the cemetery designated for a particular religious or ethnic group. This is the Catholic section. To your right in section 8 is a monument to Sarah (Sadie) Likens, Denver's first police matron.

Turn right between sections 9 and 10.

Turn right again between sections 25 and 24. Just to the right of the heavily eroded red sandstone marker is a small granite marker for Aunt Clara Brown, who was born a slave and freed in 1857. She came to Denver in 1859 and ran a successful laundry business for miners; by then she was in her 60s. She is honored with a stained glass window at the Colorado State Capitol Building (see Walk 1).

Veer left as the path goes to the cemetery's most northeastern corner.

Turn right to walk south between sections 27 and 21. On your left are the small white military grave markers—many of which simply read Unknown—of the Grand Army of the Republic Cemetery. Notable here is the grave of Capt. Silas Soule (found to the right of the flagpole in the third row), who testified against Col. John Chivington in a review of the Sand Creek Massacre (see Walk 7).

At section 20, veer left to walk with section 28 on your left and section 20 on your right.

Then veer right to walk with section 2 on your right and section 20 and the property line fence on your left. In section 20 is the marker for Barney Ford, who was born a slave and the son of his white owner in Virginia. Ford came to Colorado and repeatedly tried to make it as a miner, but African Americans were not allowed to own mine claims, Student points out. He became a successful businessman as owner of restaurants and hotels in Denver, and his prominent role in gaining rights for African Americans earned him a stained glass portrait in the Colorado State Capitol Building (see Walk 1).

When you reach the intersection near the office again, look to your right to section 6. You will see the marker for John Long Routt, who served as the last governor of the Colorado Territory before statehood and then was elected as Colorado's first state governor in 1876. He was mayor of Denver from 1883 to 1885, then reelected as state governor in 1891. Routt County, Colorado, is named for him.

The walk ends at the office on your left.

Before you head back to the living in downtown, stop and explore this little corner of Denver. Artists are modern-day pioneers, and when neighborhoods like LoDo and the Highlands got developed and rents increased in the 1990s, creative types looked northeast to the empty warehouses and industrial zones of Globeville and the northern edge of the Denver city limits. Today it's called RiNo, short for River North. See Walk 13 for a tour.

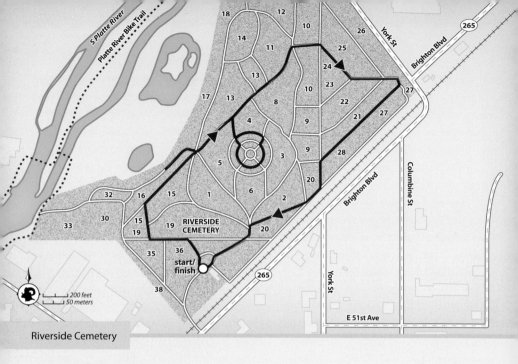

Point of Interest

1 **Riverside Cemetery** 5201 Brighton Blvd., friendsofriversidecemetery.org or fairmount-cemetery.com

13 RiNo:
Art and Food and Music

Above: The Infinite Monkey Theorem offers tours and tasting events.   photo courtesy of Visit Denver

BOUNDARIES: Downing St., Larimer St., Broadway
DISTANCE: 1 mile
DIFFICULTY: Easy
PARKING: On street, free meters on Sundays
PUBLIC TRANSIT: The RTD Route 12 bus runs along Downing St. or the light-rail D line goes to
   Downing St. & 30th, or denverbcycle.com.

The River North Arts District (RiNo) encompasses a large, formerly industrial section of the city that borders the South Platte River. This walk is just one small part of the greater boundary area that has gone from warehouses to galleries and restaurants. Frankly, it's the most walkable part of RiNo I could find, as those cool old warehouses don't all have sidewalks out front—which you will see on part of this walk. It has been argued that this area is more accurately part of the Five Points neighborhood (see Walk 14), but more and more it's being embraced as part of the developing greater RiNo area. So, let's see if I can clear this up: artists Hadley Hooper and Tracy Weil pioneered an arts community in the industrial buildings north of downtown along the South Platte River, and today developers have expanded the boundaries and what is considered part of the arts community. Throughout this walk you will see evidence of artists with large murals painted on many of the historic buildings that are now bars and restaurants.

Walk Description

You can begin this walk at one end or the other of Larimer Street because it's the same both directions. I'm starting at Larimer Street and Downing Street walking south. I recommend doing this walk as a sort of progressive lunch or dinner or even bar crawl because it is one restaurant after another here. Maybe one way to do it is walk first, building up an appetite and thirst as you make notes of where you want to stop on the way back.

❶ **Fish n' Beer,** featuring oysters as well as fish with craft brews, is only open for happy hour and dinner, so keep on walking if it's your lunch hour.

The address and entrance are one block over, but one of the best places to go dancing in Denver is ❷ **Tracks,** a gay nightclub.

As you cross 35th Street, ❸ **Phil's Place** will be on your right. It seems like an original on this street, but the wood paneling and general vibe are that of a less hip era (or maybe it's come full circle to the latest trend). This family-run place has cold beer, tacos, and green chile on offer.

What started with some craft beer in Lyons, Colorado (a small town between Boulder and Rocky Mountain National Park to the west), has evolved into a regional food empire with a small outpost here: ❹ **Oskar Blues Chuburger,** and alongside it is ❺ **Hotbox Roasters.** Start your day with coffee and a doughnut at Hotbox, then mosey back at lunch for a bison, pork, or salmon burger and cold brew at Chuburger.

A new way to enjoy your pasta is found at ❻ **Dio Mio,** where they have a frequently changing menu of handmade pastas with everything from squid ink to jalapeño.

❼ **The Infinite Monkey Theorem** could be the reason you come to this neighborhood in the first place. It's an urban winery—complete with an annual stomping of the grapes. Food trucks round out the offerings so you can make a night of it. Plan your visit with a tour or tasting event.

I love the ivy-covered walls of the patio for ❽ **The Populist.** It's such a charming spot for a special night out for upscale "American" cuisine, which is a mix of seafood, lamb, and pasta.

If you're living in the neighborhood, you might stop in ❾ **OKHI** for that retro item your place needs—you know, like a record player, drinking glass, or book.

Backstory: Art, What Art?

The RiNo Art District is within what is now known as the RiNo neighborhood, and is in fact what got the ball rolling in terms of changing this part of Denver. There are dozens of art galleries and studios to be found, but it's not the most walkable area in parts. Instead, go to rinoartdistrict.org for a guide and map to find the various art studios and spaces. Highlights include Weilworks, Redline, Plinth Gallery, and William Matthews.

For a really affordable old school Mexican meal, go to ❿ **La Casa de Manuel** for a "wet" (aka smothered with green chile sauce) burrito. What they lack in a stylish exterior they make up for with a hearty meal.

⓫ **Bar Fausto** is more than a bar. You can have a surprisingly sophisticated meal here of rabbit, oysters, and bone marrow, all paired with a huge selection of cocktails.

It's the new normal: cocktail bar + food trucks = the place to be. ⓬ **Finn's Manor** is kind of a combination of other places on this street, as the owners are also connected to The Populist and Crema. They serve beer, wine, and cocktails in a space that feels more Cajun than western with bright colors and an inviting patio.

What seems to me to be the most popular coffee shop on the street is ⓭ **Crema**, with its fishbowl corner location, friendly staff, spot-on coffee (latte, espresso, what have you), and delectable menu of salads and sandwiches.

There is no shortage of craft breweries in Colorado or even on this street, but you won't be sorry if you spend time at ⓮ **Our Mutual Friend Brewing Company.** Come for a cold beer, stay for the food truck eats and tunes. Like many of the old brick buildings along this street, the brewery's building is adorned with colorful original artwork—in this case, kaleidoscopic human figures against a blue backdrop.

Amid all of the bars, wineries, and breweries is a historic church, ⓯ **Sacred Heart Catholic Church,** which has been here since 1879. Mass is still offered in both English and Spanish. Take a few minutes to go inside and read more about the history of the church.

I've mentioned Denver B-cycle throughout this book as a way to get around town, to and from walks. Their headquarters are right here, so drop in or drop off your bike.

One place I like to come listen to and see bands is ⓰ **Larimer Lounge,** an intimate space to see local and touring bands. Just around the corner is ⓱ **The Meadowlark Bar,** a subterranean space with live music nightly. Before the Lumineers were playing Red Rocks Amphitheatre (see Walk 27), they were playing here.

Look left. **⑱ Cold Crush** is on the corner directly across the street. What sets this bar apart is that it's devoted to hip-hop music with DJs mixing old and new styles.

Cross 27th Street to arrive at the **⑲ Denver Central Market,** where you can drop in for a meal or a drink—or buy the ingredients to make your own at home.

Walk to 26th Street. If you were to turn right here you would be on Walnut Street, which is worth visiting. However, Walnut Street doesn't have a continuous sidewalk like Larimer Street, so I'll just make recommendations. You'll find Osaka Ramen for yummy Japanese food (save room for dessert), Jiberish men's boutique, 10 Barrel Brewing Company, and then at about 28th Street is Stem Ciders, with hard ciders and live music, Epic Brewing Company at about 30th Street, and the Walnut Room with late-night pizzas between 31st and 32nd.

Let's keep going on this walk of culinary possibilities! For modern Japanese, step into **⑳ Sushi Rama**—so colorful and with a conveyor belt in the center of the bar and tables with plates of sushi rolling by. Next up is **㉑ Il Posto,** which relocated from the Uptown neighborhood to RiNo, expecting that their loyal customers will follow to keep up with the ever-changing seasonal Italian menu.

One more block to go. **㉒ Port Side** is a coffee shop with a full breakfast and a lunch menu too. Another retail store mixed in here is **㉓ Topo Designs,** which makes outdoor gear and apparel for men and women.

And while not the last restaurant in the area, the last on my list of recommendations during this walk is **㉔ Los Chingones,** an upscale Mexican eatery that offers indoor and outdoor seating.

Once you've reached Broadway it's time to turn around and walk back to your car or bike or bus. Before you do though, look across the street for the rhinoceros sculpture, *Rhino,* by Mike Whiting (2010).

Points of Interest

❶ Fish n' Beer 3510 Larimer St., 303-248-3497, fishnbeerdenver.com

❷ Tracks 3500 Walnut St., 303-863-7326, tracksdenver.com

❸ Phil's Place 3463 Larimer St., 303-298-1559

❹ Oskar Blues Chuburger 3490 Larimer St., 720-668-9167, oskarbluesfooderies.com

❺ Hotbox Roasters 3450 Larimer St., 720-668-9167, hotboxroasters.com

❻ Dio Mio 3264 Larimer St., 303-562-1965, diomiopasta.com

❼ The Infinite Monkey Theorem 3200 Larimer St., 303-736-8376, theinfinitemonkeytheorem.com

❽ The Populist 3163 Larimer St., 720-432-3163, thepopulistdenver.com

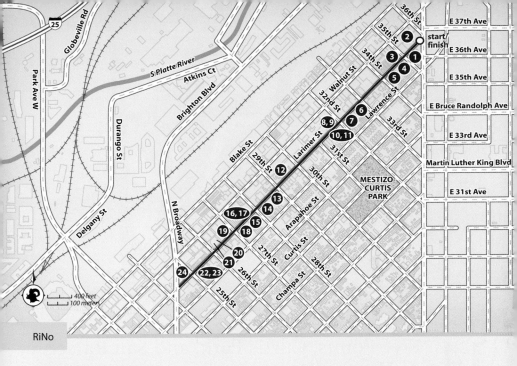

RiNo

9 **OKHI** 3151 Larimer St., 303-619-4386

10 **La Casa de Manuel** 3158 Larimer St., 303-295-1752

11 **Bar Fausto** 3126 Larimer St., 720-445-9691, barfausto.com

12 **Finn's Manor** 2927 Larimer St., finnsmanor.co

13 **Crema** 2862 Larimer St., 720-284-9648, cremacoffeehouse.net

14 **Our Mutual Friend Brewing Company** 2810 Larimer St., 303-296-3441, omfbeer.com

15 **Sacred Heart Catholic Church** 2760 Larimer St., 303-294-9830

16 **Larimer Lounge** 2721 Larimer St., 303-291-1007, larimerlounge.com

17 **The Meadowlark Bar** 2701 Larimer St., 303-293-0251, meadowlarkbar.com

18 **Cold Crush** 2700 Larimer St., 303-292-1906, coldcrush.net

19 **Denver Central Market** 2669 Larimer St., denvercentralmarket.com

20 **Sushi Rama** 2615 Larimer St., 720-476-4643, sushi-rama.com

21 **Il Posto** 2601 Larimer St., 303-394-1100, ilpostodenver.com

22 **Port Side** 2500 Larimer St. #103, 720-549-0622, portsidedenver.com

23 **Topo Designs** 2500 Larimer St., 303-954-8420, topodesigns.com

24 **Los Chingones** 2463 Larimer St., 303-295-0686, loschingonesmexican.com

14 Five Points, Curtis Park, and San Rafael
Historic Districts: A Hub of African American History

BOUNDARIES: 24th St., Curtis St., Downing St., 22nd St.
DISTANCE: Approx. 2.5 miles
DIFFICULTY: Easy
PARKING: Free parking is available on many streets.
PUBLIC TRANSIT: The RTD light-rail D line goes to 30th and Downing and makes stops along Welton St.; Denver B-cycle (denverbcycle.com) has a station at 27th Ave. and Welton St.

This walk combines three historic districts located about one mile from downtown Denver: the Five Points commercial district, once called the "Harlem of the West" and Denver's first African American neighborhood; Curtis Park, which is Denver's oldest residential neighborhood; and the San Rafael Historic District, with its turn-of-the-century homes and grand churches. The entire area has gone through the highest highs to the lowest lows over the years and is still in the process of renewal. This walk includes three institutions devoted to African American history—in this neighborhood and well beyond—as well as historical buildings, churches, and homes, all in the shadow of downtown skyscrapers.

Walk Description

This walk begins with a recommendation to not just begin your tour in front of the ❶ **Blair-Caldwell African American Research Library** (a branch of the Denver Public Library) at Welton Street and 24th Avenue, but to go inside. The third floor of the library is an exhibit space tracing the history of African Americans to the West and also has replicas of a barber shop—and the story of the barber and his family escaping slavery and coming to Denver—of the Roxy Theater with video and music, and a replica of the mayoral office of Mayor Wellington E. Webb, Denver's first African American mayor, who served three terms from 1991 to 2003. The Wellington E. Webb Municipal Office Building is on Walk 2. A "Leadership Gallery" tells the stories of numerous African American leaders from Denver and Colorado. On the second floor are archives and the research library.

The library opened in 2003 as part of the revitalization efforts for this area. It is named for Omar Blair, the first African American to head Denver's School Board, and Elvin Caldwell, Denver's first African American city councilman.

❷ **Sonny Lawson Park** on the west side of the library is where author Jack Kerouac spent an evening watching a baseball game, which he wrote about in his classic, *On the Road*. Kerouac's pal Neal Cassady grew up in this neighborhood. It was the first ballpark in Denver to host Negro League games. Sonny Lawson was a local African American businessman.

Walk north on Welton Street from the library.

Turn left on 25th Street to walk west. This portion of the walk takes you through the Curtis Park neighborhood, which was Denver's first "streetcar suburb" when horse-drawn cable cars brought people from downtown up to 27th and Champa Streets. Houses in this neighborhood date back to the 1870s, with many of them built in the early 1880s. At the corner of 25th and California Streets is the former ❸ **First German Society of the Methodist Episcopal Church**, built in 1887, and is now the Agape Christian Church. The house at 2445 California Street on your left was built in 1879, as was the home at 2461.

Detailed history and architectural details of the houses in the area are given in *Curtis Park: Denver's Oldest Neighborhood* by William Allen West. West points out that as soon as water was made available to Brown's Bluff, now called Capitol Hill (see Walk 1), wealthy citizens pulled out of Curtis Park and built new mansions on the hilltop before 1900. The heyday of fancy houses in Curtis Park was short lived, and it became a middle-class area with a mix of immigrants and then a lower-middle-class area with Italianate and Queen Anne–style mansions turned into boardinghouses.

At this juncture you can walk three blocks to Curtis Street and take a right to walk to 30th Street. Or take a right on California Street, walk one block, turn left on 26th Street, then right on Stout Street and walk one block. Turn left on 27th Street, walk one block to Champa Street, and turn right to walk one block to 28th Street. Turn left on 28th, then right on Curtis Street, staying on Curtis Street until you reach 30th Street.

❹ **Mestizo-Curtis Park** at 3000 Curtis Street is, as you might guess given the age of the houses, the city's oldest park. Thanks to revitalization efforts and dollars, there is a playground and new garden areas in the park. Take a right and walk east on 30th Street back to California Street.

Turn left on California Street and walk one block to the ❺ **Black American West Museum** on your left at the corner of 31st and California Streets. The museum is in the one-time home of Dr. Justina Ford, the first African American woman doctor in Colorado. (Dr. Ford's husband was the Reverend John E. Ford, minister at the Zion Baptist Church from 1899 to 1906.) Dr. Ford came to Denver in 1902 and lived in this house, although it was several blocks away where it was originally built in 1888. The house was saved from demolition and relocated in 1983. The museum has a few exhibits, including one with more details about Dr. Ford, and also displays about Buffalo Soldiers and rodeo cowboys like Deadwood Dick and Bill Pickett.

Note: If you've had enough walking for one day, the RTD light-rail station is directly across the street from the museum. You can take the light-rail train back to the library at 24th and Welton Streets or into downtown.

Turn around and walk back to 30th Street, then continue east to Welton Street, turning right at the vintage Tivoli sign painted on the side of the brick building. Through the 1950s, Welton Street was the main commercial strip for Five Points, with three newspapers, nightclubs, movie theatres, hotels, dentists, barbers, hatters, and many other businesses that catered to the African American population. For many reasons since then—desegregation, crime, a slumping economy all among them—Five Points has become a neighborhood without a community as it slowly gentrifies and storefronts sit empty. You'll hear the ding-ding of the light-rail train as it makes stops along the street.

An annual Juneteenth Festival was revived in the last few years and fills the street one summer weekend with food vendors, music, and special celebrations to honor the end of slavery in the United States.

Just before the neighborhood's namesake five-point intersection at Washington Street/Welton Street/27th Street is one of the few new businesses on this street: ❻ **The Rolling Pin,** a cheery little bakeshop where you can't go wrong on choosing croissants or cakes.

At the corner of Washington and Welton Streets is the **❼ Rossonian Hotel** (built in 1912 as the Baxter Hotel, then changed to the Rossonian in 1929). The Rossonian was Denver's jazz mecca from the 1930s through the 1950s, with big names like Duke Ellington, Nat King Cole, Billie Holliday, Louis Armstrong, and other greats playing here. Jack Kerouac and Neal Cassady were jazz lovers and were known to frequent the Rossonian too. It has been sitting vacant for ages and remains full of potential, but perhaps by the time you are taking this walk it will be a working hotel again.

Walk south on Washington Street with the Rossonian on your right side. As you approach 25th Avenue, look left to see **❽ Denver Firehouse Station No 3,** which was built in 1931 and is still a fully functioning firehouse. The city created the only African American fire station to serve the Five Points area in 1893. The fire department was integrated in the 1950s, and Denver's first African American fire chief was named in 2001.

On your right on the triangular corner of the block is the **❾ Stiles African American Heritage Center,** which has many African American artifacts on display and also provides educational workshops, reenactments, and other history lessons.

Continue walking south on Washington Street to 23rd Avenue. At the corner is a one-time Presbyterian church that was built here in 1883.

Turn left on 23rd Avenue to walk to Ogden Street. You will see the **❿ Belltower Residences at San Rafael** on the corner. This 1915 building was once home to the New Hope Baptist Church and was recently converted to four very swanky condominiums.

Turn right on Ogden Street and walk to 22nd Avenue. Turn left. On this corner are the **⓫ Sanctuary Lofts,** once the Scott Methodist Church.

Turn right on Emerson Street and walk to 24th Avenue. At 24th Street look right to see the **⓬ Zion Baptist Church,** built in 1892. According to Michelle Pearson in *Historic Sacred Places of Denver,* the Zion Baptist congregation is considered one of the oldest African American congregations in the United States, founded in 1865. This church was built for the congregation of the Calvary Baptist Church and bought by the Zion congregation in 1911.

Zion Baptist Church is home to one of the country's first African American congregations.

Backstory: Not for Everyone

Denver was a segregated city. The Rossonian was not only famous for its jazz music but also for welcoming African Americans who could not stay in the other hotels downtown. When musicians came to town to play a show, they were told they could stay at the Rossonian for free if they played some music in the lobby—after their other concerts.

Smith Lake in Washington Park (see Walk 20) was unofficially for whites only, writes Nancy Widman in her book *Washington Park*. The exception was Japanese people, who were officially barred. One day in 1932 a large group of African Americans came to Smith Lake to swim, and a small riot broke out.

And in *Denver's Riverside Cemetery: Where History Lies*, author Annette Student tells of how former-slave turned businessman Barney Ford came to Colorado to seek his fortune in the mines, like so many other men.

"Although Blacks were allowed to own land at the time, they were not allowed to file on a mining claim or a homestead," she writes. Ford filed several claims on mines, only to have them jumped by white men. Ford went on to become a prosperous and highly respected hotel and restaurant owner in Denver.

Turn left when Emerson Street meets 26th Avenue. You will find yourself back at the five-point intersection and the Rossonian once again as you reach Welton Street. On your right is ⑬ **Rosenberg's Bagels and Delicatessen,** one of the few new businesses in this neighborhood. As historic neighborhoods like the Highlands have exploded with change in recent years, this area has had a slower renewal.

Turn left and walk south on Welton Street. On your right you will pass the former Casino Cabaret, now ⑭ **Cervantes' Masterpiece,** two concert spaces for bands that are a far cry from the jazz classics of the past. Next up the ⑮ **Roxy Theatre,** a former movie theatre and dance club, is now a live music venue too.

The walk ends where it began at the library.

Points of Interest

① **Blair-Caldwell African American Research Library** 2401 Welton St., 720-865-2401, history.denverlibrary.org/blair

② **Sonny Lawson Park** 2300 Welton St.

Five Points, Curtis Park, and San Rafael Historic Districts

3 First German Society of the Methodist Episcopal Church/Agape Christian Church
2501 California St., 303-296-2452, agapechristianchurch.org

4 Mestizo-Curtis Park 3000 Curtis St.

5 The Black American West Museum 3091 California St., 720-242-7428, bawmhc.org

6 The Rolling Pin 2716 Welton St., 720-708-3026, therollingpinbakeshop.com

7 Rossonian Building 2650 Welton St.

8 Denver Firehouse Station No 3 2500 Washington St., 720-913-3473, denvergov.org

9 Stiles African American Heritage Center 2607 Glenarm Pl., 303-294-0597, stilesheritagecenter.org

10 Belltower Residences 23rd & Ogden Sts.

11 Sanctuary Lofts 22nd & Emerson St.

12 Zion Baptist Church 933 E. 24th Ave., 303-863-9413, zionbaptistchurchdenver.org

13 Rosenberg's Bagels and Delicatessen 725 E. 26th Ave., 720-440-9880, rosenbergsbagels.com

14 Cervantes' Masterpiece 2635 Welton St., 303-297-1772, cervantesmasterpiece.com

15 Roxy Theatre 2549 Welton St., 720-381-6420, theroxydenver.com

15 Mile High Loop:
Scenery with Altitude

Above: *Views from the Mile High Loop include City Park's Ferril Lake, the City Park Pavilion, and the peaks of the Rocky Mountains.*

BOUNDARIES: Colorado Blvd., 17th Ave., York St., 23rd Ave.
DISTANCE: 3.1 miles
DIFFICULTY: Easy
PARKING: Free parking is available around the park and in the parking lots of Denver Zoo and Denver Museum of Nature and Science.
PUBLIC TRANSIT: RTD local bus 20

Denver's newest footpath celebrates the city's claim to fame: being 5,280 feet above sea level, or 1 mile high. The Mile High Loop was created as a way for pedestrians and runners to enjoy exercising along a trail that hits the elevation of 5,280 feet throughout City Park. The graveled path takes you past lakes, ponds, fountains, playgrounds, statues, gardens, and the Denver Museum of Nature and Science and features one of the best views of the Rocky Mountains in the city. The

Mile High Loop is certainly not the only path in City Park, and while it traverses paved roads and bicycle paths, it provides another way for even locals to enjoy Denver's largest park. The time of day and the seasons will affect what you can see along the way—from blossoming trees to an electric light fountain and much more.

Note: As with other park walks, be aware that this trail crosses roads within the park. Always cross roads cautiously because cars have access to the park as well.

Walk Description

Begin the walk at the Mile High Loop sign, to the west of Ferril Lake and the Pavilion. ❶ **City Park** is a sprawling 370 acres but is divided in half by 23rd Avenue, leaving the City Park Golf Course taking up one half on the north side. You should be standing on a small island between a road and a parking lot with Ferril Lake to one side and Duck Lake on the other. There is a historical sign here with more details.

Cross the parking lot and walk to the trail where it begins below the rim of Ferril Lake. Ferril Lake is named after Colorado's poet laureate of 1979, Thomas Ferril, who enjoyed walks around this lake with his dog.

Walk north on the trail, with the walls of the ❷ **Denver Zoo** on your left. Duck Lake, which is on your left too, is part of the Denver Zoo and is often filled with a variety of birds.

As you leave the lake and enter the meadow below the ❸ **Denver Museum of Nature and Science,** you will pass the lilac and crab apple garden on your left. This is so pretty in the spring when the pink, white, and purple fragrant blossoms are at their peak.

Just before the trail curves is a mile-high marker across the path. It's a quirk of Denver to have these random 5,280-foot markers in a few special spots around the city, and people love to have their photos taken next to them. Other markers are found on the steps of the Colorado State Capitol Building (Walk 1) and along the purple row of seats at Coors Field (Walk 5).

Follow the trail as it curves right and becomes parallel with the museum. The west side of the museum looks out over City Park. This is a great place for a little detour up the steps to the museum. Look west and take in the spectacular Rocky Mountain view.

Kid Tip: If it's summer, you'll be enjoying the rose gardens and the ❹ **H2Odyssey Inter-active Water Fountain** that flanks this side of the museum as well. That's right, interactive as in walk right into the huge sprays of water shooting up.

Kid Tip: If you want to make your walk a little shorter, ask your parents to run downhill to the right to a playground. If they say no, don't worry because there is another (bigger!) playground later in the walk too.

From the museum begin walking south, or go to your left, making sure to stay on the gravel-and-dirt path even when it is just a shoulder to a concrete sidewalk. The path slopes downhill past the new DeBoer Waterway, which is a lovely replication of natural mountain streams.

After you pass a wooden totem pole, you will be on the Boettcher Plaza just outside the newest addition to the museum, Morgridge Family Exploration Center. Iridescent Cloud is a sculpture by artists Laura Haddad and Tom Drugan. This treelike sculpture is one part of a whole piece of art. I love how it reflects the light and looks different during each season and time of day. Keep walking toward Colorado Boulevard, and now you are actually standing on the rest of the art installation, Spectral Band, sort of a modern pot of gold at the end of the rainbow, or rainbow brick road.

Hop over the dividers to reach the sidewalk parallel to Colorado Boulevard. This is the most urban part of the loop as you walk perpendicular to busy Colorado Boulevard. In spring yellow tulips are in bloom alongside the path.

Go right at the corner of Colorado Boulevard and 17th Avenue as the path takes a welcome turn back into the calmer realm of the park's trees and flowers.

As the path slips between Little Lake and the tip of 24-acre Ferril Lake, honking geese and other birdsongs begin to take over the city sounds. The small island in Ferril Lake is home to black-crowned night herons and double-crested cormorants—as well as the obligatory geese. A bit farther on at the lake's west end, you can rent pedal boats to take out on the lake (wheelfunrentals .com) or bicycles and surreys to ride around the park during summer months only.

Between mid-May and mid-September, you can see the Darlington Electric Fountain put on a show during free weekly jazz concerts (cityparkjazz.org).

Just after you pass the soccer fields you will see the East High School campus on your left across the street from the park. This is another 5,280-foot point on the walk. The basin of Thatcher Memorial Fountain (also called Colorado Memorial Fountain) on your right is also 5,280 feet above sea level.

Across the City Park Esplanade is the old Lowenstein Theatre, now renovated to house the ❺ **Tattered Cover Bookstore** with a coffee and pastry shop, and next door is ❻ **Twist & Shout** music store and the Denver Film Society (see Walk 17).

Curve right on the trail where mature evergreen trees provide shade along the path up ahead and parallel York Street. In spring the pink and white tree blossoms are abundant in the park, and this stretch feels like a stroll in a public botanical garden.

Backstory: Isn't It Beautiful?

In the early 1900s, Denver's popular Mayor Robert Speer was determined to turn the arid plains of this growing new city into the "Paris of America," as he was inspired by the City Beautiful Movement that was transforming urban planning across the country then.

To show off his "Denver the City Beautiful," Mayor Speer commissioned a Darlington Electric Fountain—with nine colored lights and 25 water jets—to be built in City Park's Ferril Lake. Joseph Addison Thatcher, founder of the Denver National Bank, donated the fountain to the city of Denver in 1918. Sculptor Lorado Zadac Taft created the single female figure to stand for Colorado and three smaller figures to represent the virtues of the state: loyalty, learning, and love.

Time was not kind to the fountain, and it went unused for decades until once again a mayor found himself inspired by politics (of course!). When he was Denver's mayor, John Hickenlooper (who has since been Colorado governor) had the Darlington Electric Fountain and the Thatcher Memorial Statue spruced up in time for the city to host the Democratic National Convention. The Darlington Electric Fountain had to be completely rebuilt but is now serving its original purpose again to put on an impressive water and light show on hot summer nights.

The Graham-Bible House to the left is historically where park superintendents lived and is named after two former City Park superintendents.

At 22nd Avenue you pass the historic McClellan Gateway to the park.

At the corner of 23rd Avenue the trail loops around and you begin to head back toward the museum.

Kid Tip: Toward the end of your walk, there is a big playground with swings, a lot of climbing structures, and more. It's the one I always ask my mom to take me to when we come to this park.

The ❼ **Dr. Martin Luther King Jr. Memorial Monument** by Ed Dwight is on your right as you approach the peach-colored pavilion and bandstand. You can leave the trail to see the monument up close and read a large plaque to the south side. Before you reach the pavilion, you will see a statue of poet Robert Burns to the left.

The loop ends just ahead to the left of the pavilion. You can combine this walk with either Walk 16 by walking east on Montview Boulevard from the east side of the Denver Museum of Nature and Science or east on 23rd Avenue or with Walk 17 by heading west on 17th Avenue.

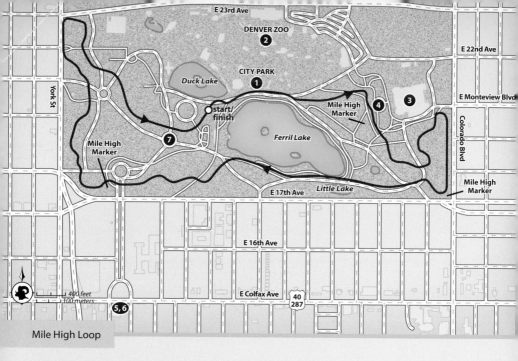

Points of Interest

1. **City Park** 3300 E. 17th Ave., 303-331-4113, denvergov.org

2. **Denver Zoo** 2300 Steele St., 303-376-4800, denverzoo.org

3. **Denver Museum of Nature and Science** 2001 Colorado Blvd., 303-322-7009, dmns.org

4. **H2Odyssey Interactive Water Fountain**

5. **Tattered Cover Bookstore** 2526 E. Colfax Ave., 303-322-7727, tatteredcover.com

6. **Twist & Shout** 2508 E. Colfax Ave., 303-722-1943, twistandshout.com

7. **Dr. Martin Luther King Jr. Memorial Monument**

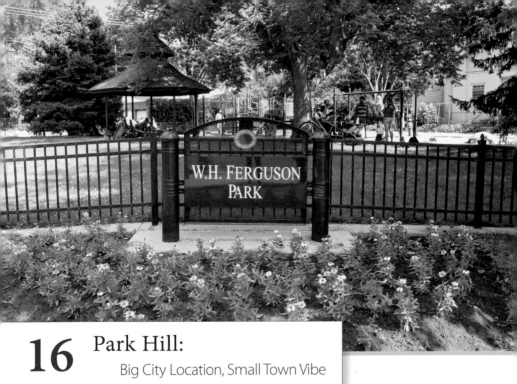

16 Park Hill:
Big City Location, Small Town Vibe

Above: W. H. Ferguson Park is popular with neighborhood kids.

BOUNDARIES: 23rd Ave., Forest St., Montview Blvd., Dexter St.
DISTANCE: 1 mile
DIFFICULTY: Easy
PARKING: Free on-street parking
PUBLIC TRANSIT: RTD 20 bus makes stops on Montview Blvd.

In the late 1800s Denver's downtown was a place of saloons, brothels, and crowded, filthy streets. Those who could afford it seemed always on the lookout for the next best neighborhood that put distance between them and downtown. According to *Denver: Mining Camp to Metropolis,* by authors Stephen J. Leonard and Thomas J. Noel, "Park Hill, a haven for the upper crust on the high ground east of City Park, was platted in 1887." The original plan was for a racetrack surrounded by "a posh residential subdivision," but that didn't come to fruition. Next it was sold as "Denver's

Largest Restricted Residence District" with a brochure that "declared that Capitol Hill has been spoiled as a residential area by the intrusion of apartments and commercial buildings." Today the neighborhood seems much like those early planners had hoped (minus one racetrack).

Park Hill is indeed one of Denver's most desirable places to live in the city, thanks to its proximity just east of City Park and some of Denver's most popular attractions, the Denver Zoo and the Denver Museum of Nature and Science. Wide tree-lined streets with big to grand homes fill the neighborhood that is also anchored by some small business districts that make it that much more pedestrian friendly. It's also home to a few large and distinctive churches that are another aspect of the strong community bonds here. Stroll among the houses, past families playing in the park, and stop in and have a bite to eat and a cup of coffee as you get to know Park Hill.

Walk Description

Begin this walk at the corner of Montview Boulevard and Dexter Street at the Park Hill Branch Library. Montview Boulevard westbound ends at the Denver Museum of Nature and Science on the northern edge of City Park (see Walk 15).

❶ **The Park Hill Branch Library** is another Carnegie-funded library, this time with hints of Spanish design. Inside there are comfortable chairs near the original fireplace, and big arched windows let in plenty of natural light.

Walk north on Dexter Street. At the corner of 22nd Avenue and Dexter is ❷ **St. Thomas Episcopal Church,** which looks like it belongs somewhere in California with its Spanish Colonial design. The church was started in 1908, then the first building was erected here in 1916, and because of their growing parish, it was expanded in 1930. Inside is a handmade tile floor.

Continue walking north on Dexter Street to 23rd Avenue. So many elements combine to bring Park Hill residents together at this intersection. ❸ **W. H. Ferguson Park**—locally referred to as "Turtle Park" because of the very popular turtle sculpture kids climb on—on one corner always has kids swinging or just running around.

❹ **Spinelli's Bakery & Café** has locally made Sweet Action Ice Cream, sandwiches, coffee, just so much to keep walking off later!

❺ **Park Hill Community Bookstore** is a volunteer-run nonprofit bookstore, likely the only one in Denver. They have both new and used books for members and nonmembers with a good selection of all kinds of books for any age.

Across the street is ❻ **Spinelli's Market,** where the owners greet every customer who comes in—usually by name like on *Cheers.* Spinelli's is like the old-fashioned markets that used to be in every neighborhood, with your basic staples for the pantry or fridge, but with the added bonus of a really good deli and some gourmet foods too. In addition, they have their own line of Italian sauces for sale here.

Spinelli's is in the same building as ❼ **The Cherry Tomato,** an Italian restaurant, that is—you guessed it—a neighborhood favorite for dinner. Formerly a church and then a drugstore, this building anchors the block, and there are always people coming and going from these popular businesses.

Turn right and walk east one block on 23rd Avenue.

Turn right and walk south on Dahlia Street.

Turn left on 22nd Avenue and walk to Forest Street. As you wander along looking at the houses in Park Hill, keep in mind that the Greater Park Hill Community Inc. (greaterparkhill.org) hosts an annual home tour in September and garden tour in June.

St. Thomas Episcopal Church

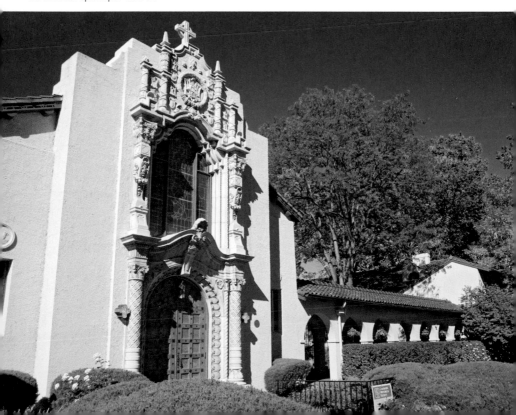

Backstory: But Wait, There's More

One mile east on 23rd Avenue from the Spinelli's Bakery & Café is another very popular Park Hill bakery, Cake Crumbs (2216 Kearney St., 303-861-4912, cake-crumbs.com), in a one-block commercial district that gives people who live at that end of the neighborhood some places to walk to also. Known for their sweets, Cake Crumbs also has a savory menu for lunch. When it's time for dinner, Tables (2267 Kearney St., 303-388-0299, tablesonkearney.com) draws people from beyond the neighborhood for its seasonally changing menu. Or, if you just want fast and casual, Oblio's Pizzeria (6115 E. 22nd Ave., 303-321-1511, obliospizza.com).

Turn right and walk to Montview Boulevard. At the corner of Forest Street and Montview Boulevard is ❽ **Park Hill United Methodist Church.** It is another example of the Spanish Colonial Revival architecture, yet very different—and a lot bigger—than St. Thomas Episcopal Church earlier on the walk. This church was built in 1924 and was added onto in 1956 to accommodate a growing parish. Part of this space is shared with Temple Micah, "a Reform synagogue."

You can extend the walk and enjoy the grand homes in this neighborhood by walking south on Forest Street as it becomes Forest Parkway. These large grassy islands are like parks for each block, where I've seen families having picnics and tossing the football around. The luxury of open space! Do a loop and come back after you reach 17th Avenue to resume this walk on Montview Boulevard going left.

If you didn't do the detour, turn right to walk west on Montview Boulevard from the Park Hill United Methodist Church. On the south side or opposite side of the street you will see the ❾ **Blessed Sacrament Catholic Church,** built in 1912.

Just before the Park Hill Library but on the south side of Montview Boulevard is ❿ **Montview Boulevard Presbyterian Church,** perhaps *the* landmark church of the neighborhood. The first stone chapel was built on this site in 1910 (they had previously been in a wood-frame schoolhouse at this location), with three additions since then. The church is known as much for its political and community actions as for its worship services. In the 1960s, during racial integration in Denver, Montview's pastor took a stand and asked parishioners to "sign a non-discriminatory pledge when buying and selling real estate," according to Michelle Pearson in *Historic Sacred Places of Denver.* They also opened a racially integrated preschool during that time, and Dr. Martin Luther King Jr. spoke at Montview in 1964.

End the walk back at or near Park Hill Library. This walk can be combined with Walk 15 by walking several blocks west on Montview Boulevard to Colorado Boulevard.

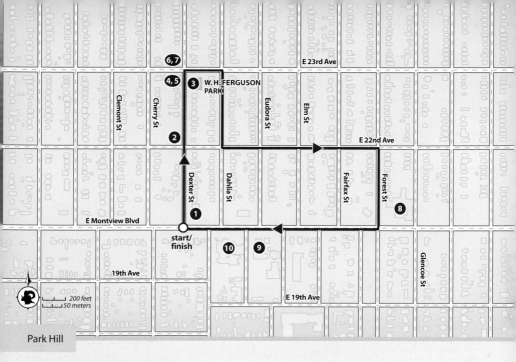

Points of Interest

1. **Park Hill Branch Library** 4705 Montview Blvd., 720-865-0250, denverlibrary.org
2. **St. Thomas Episcopal Church** 2201 Dexter St., 303-388-4395, saintthomasdenver.org
3. **W. H. Ferguson Park** 4716 E. 23rd Ave.
4. **Spinelli's Bakery & Café** 4628 E. 23rd Ave., 720-424-6048
5. **Park Hill Community Bookstore** 4620 E. 23rd Ave., 303-355-8508
6. **Spinelli's Market** 4631 E. 23rd Ave., 303-329-8143, spinellismarket.com
7. **The Cherry Tomato** 4645 E. 23rd Ave., 303-377-1914, cherrytomatodenver.com
8. **Park Hill United Methodist Church** 5209 Montview Blvd., 303-322-1867, phumc.org
9. **Blessed Sacrament Catholic Church** 4900 Montview Blvd., 303-355-7361, blessedsacrament.net
10. **Montview Boulevard Presbyterian Church** 1980 Dahlia St., 303-355-1651, montview.org

17 Wyman Historic District and Uptown:
Dine on Restaurant Row and Sleep in a Castle

Above: *Castle Marne Bed and Breakfast*

BOUNDARIES: E. Colfax Ave., Vine St., Clarkson St., 17th St.
DISTANCE: 0.5 mile to 1.5 miles
DIFFICULTY: Easy
PARKING: Metered parking on Colfax Ave. and free parking on side streets
PUBLIC TRANSIT: The RTD 15 or 15L buses make frequent stops along E. Colfax Ave.

As Denver grew out from downtown and water pipes were laid to the east in the 1880s, homes were built along the city's best corridors and along side streets nearby. Colfax Avenue was a place of wealthy citizens in large and stunning mansions back then. Today's modern Wyman Historic District is bisected by the far-less-glamorous Colfax Avenue that has long since changed and lost most of its original architecture and residential homes. On this walk you will see a sweet slice of the Wyman Historic District on the north side of Colfax Avenue. In just a few charming blocks in the heart of the city you will see a small selection of homes from that bygone era before the Silver

Crash of 1893 that so changed Denver, including a castlelike inn that has been restored to that time period. Whether or not you choose to stay the night there, you can make an evening of it in this neighborhood with your pick of some of Denver's best restaurants.

Walk Description

Start this walk in front of the fountain at Colfax Avenue and Esplanade (a semicircle drive that leads to the grand East High School) and directly across the street from the ❶ Tattered Cover Bookstore, ❷ Twist & Shout, and Sie Film Center. Whether you need a cup of coffee and want to browse for books or some new tunes, or are just stretching your legs before a flick, this will be a nice place to return when you end the walk (or do one of those things before the walk instead!).

Begin walking west on E. Colfax Avenue toward Race Street, six blocks away. Although Colfax Avenue is a main east-west artery through Denver and its suburbs, the busy street is not ideal for pedestrians for many reasons. The entire Colfax Avenue is 26 miles long. Historically, E. Colfax Avenue was a desirable location for mansions of the city's wealthiest residents in the late 1800s. But, as in other parts of Denver, the Silver Crash of 1893 changed all that, and soon apartment buildings were favored over mansions, then businesses over residential, and then simply undesirable businesses. Now there are revitalized blocks along the busy road with new appeal, such as where you started with the Tattered Cover Book Store.

As you cross York Street, note that less than half a block to your right is ❸ Tacos Tequila Whiskey, one of the city's top taco bars. Just before Race Street, you will pass ❹ SAME Café and can see ❺ Pete's Kitchen across the street. SAME Café is a unique place: the name is an acronym for So All May Eat, and the concept is that customers pay what they can for their meals. It's really tasty too, with organic pizzas, sandwiches, and desserts. On the opposite corner you will see Pete's Kitchen, a longtime Denver favorite for breakfast or late-night eats for the after-hours crowd thanks to the 24-hour schedule here. The menu is diner fare with Greek options—make that anything with fries (except for salads, and then you just order a side of fries). Souvlaki with fries, gyros plate with fries, and so on.

Turn right on Race Street to walk north. The next two blocks are reminiscent of what early E. Colfax Avenue must have been like with grand mansions facing one another from both sides of the street and birds chirping in the tall trees that line the streets. That said, the first house on the left at 1515 Race Street was relocated here from its original location across from the Molly Brown House Museum (see Walk 1) in 1989. It is now home to the Lighthouse Writers Workshop, where anyone can attend seminars, readings, and other literary events all year.

As you reach the corner of 16th Avenue, you will notice the ❻ **Castle Marne Bed and Breakfast** on your right. Built in 1889 by noted architect William Lang and made of Castle Rock rhyolite, the building was lived in as a private home, then used for offices, and then abandoned and vandalized. Saved from possible demolition, it was painstakingly restored to its original days of glory and opened as a bed and breakfast in 1989.

Rest your feet and get a cup of coffee at St. Mark's Coffeehouse.

Walk one more block to 17th Avenue. Among the lovely brick mansions, you will notice a rare bungalow at 1616 Race Street on your right, built in 1912.

Just across 17th Avenue at Race Street there are a few places for refreshment: ❼ **The Thin Man** for cocktails and ❽ **St. Mark's Coffeehouse** for, well, coffee, and on nice days, the garage doors roll up and walls disappear to merge the indoor and outdoor space.

For those turning left, this walk down 17th Avenue toward downtown leaves the Wyman Historic District and becomes Uptown, also called Restaurant Row. Along the way you will see a mix of new and old apartment buildings, duplexes, and businesses.

(Turn left at 17th Avenue, or make this a much shorter walk and turn right, jumping ahead to the last four paragraphs here for directions.)

Among the recommended restaurants you will walk past are ❾ **Dos Santos Taqueria de Mexico** (I am of the belief that you can't have too many taco restaurants, so yes, two in one walk!) and ❿ **Bread n Butter** for everything southern, including whiskeys.

After crossing Park Avenue West, stop in at ⓫ **Talulah Jones** for a little something for the child in your life—a toy or book perhaps—then grab some stationery, jewelry, or something else unexpected for yourself or a friend.

At Ogden Street the house on the opposite corner is now a most fabulous spa, the ⓬ **Woodhouse Day Spa** at the Merritt House. The 10-bedroom home was built in 1886 for Senator Elmer W. Merritt, who was a founder of the Colorado Museum of Natural History (now the Denver Museum of Nature and Science, seen on Walk 14). On the same block is a house at 931 17th Avenue that was built in 1885 and designed by architect Frank Edbrooke, who is best known for designing the Brown Palace Hotel (seen on Walk 6).

At Emerson Street on the right side you will see **⓭ Watercourse,** Denver's most popular vegetarian restaurant. It too has a 17th Avenue patio for those who can't get enough Colorado sunshine.

At Clarkson Street you will see Marczyk Fine Foods, which is, yes, a grocery store, but a really good one! Its deli makes hearty sandwiches and sells refrigerated meals you can easily heat up.

Across the street from Marczyk is **⓮ Beast + Bottle,** known for its fresh farm-to-table seasonal menus and excellent wine list.

If you were to continue walking down 17th Avenue toward downtown, you would find even more restaurants to choose from, but it would make this walk very long! Turn around and walk east on 17th Avenue.

Once you pass Race Street, you will walk one block east to Vine Street, and on the opposite corner you will see the **⓯ Vine Street Pub,** with burgers and burritos on the menu, their own brew on tap, and live music every week.

Turn right on Vine Street. Much like Race Street, the next two blocks are a treasure of beautiful historic homes. Of particular interest are the homes on the right side just before 16th Avenue, which are in the Prairie architectural style that architect Frank Lloyd Wright made popular.

As you cross 16th Avenue looking left you will see East High School, which is also visible

Grab a bite to eat, then keep walking!

during Walk 14. The building on the corner is an example of Streamline Moderne architecture, particularly with its round windows on one side. You can walk up to 16th Avenue, crossing York Street and Josephine Street, to East High School (rather than return to Colfax Avenue and retrace your steps) and turn right on Esplanade to return to the fountain and the beginning of the walk. East High School was built at its current location in 1925 and became a Denver Historic Landmark in 1991. The clock tower continues to keep time!

This walk can be combined with Walk 15 by walking east up 17th Avenue or with Walk 18 by going south on York Street or by turning left instead of right when you reach East High School.

Wyman Historic District and Uptown

Points of Interest

1. **Tattered Cover Book Store** 2526 E. Colfax Ave., 303-322-7727, tatteredcover.com
2. **Twist & Shout** 2508 E. Colfax Ave., 303-722-1943, twistandshout.com
3. **Tacos Tequila Whiskey** 1415 York St., 720-475-1337, tacostequilawhiskey.com
4. **SAME Café** 2023 E. Colfax Ave., 720-530-6853, soallmayeat.org
5. **Pete's Kitchen** 1962 E. Colfax Ave., 303-321-3139, petesrestaurants.com
6. **Castle Marne Bed and Breakfast** 1572 Race St., 303-331-0621, castlemarne.com
7. **The Thin Man** 2015 E. 17th Ave., 303-320-7814
8. **St. Mark's Coffeehouse** 2019 E. 17th Ave., 303-322-8384, stmarkscoffeehouse.com
9. **Dos Santos** 1475 E. 17th Ave., 303-386-3509, dossantosdenver.com
10. **Bread n Butter** 1618 E. 17th Ave., 303-322-0898, breadnbutterdenver.com
11. **Talulah Jones** 1122 E. 17th Ave., 303-832-1230, talulahonline.com
12. **Woodhouse Day Spa** 941 E. 17th Ave., 303-813-8488, denver.woodhousespas.com
13. **Watercourse** 210 E. 13th Ave., 303-318-9844, watercoursefoods.com
14. **Beast + Bottle** 719 E. 17th Ave., 303-623-3223, beastandbottle.com
15. **Vine Street Pub** 1700 Vine St., 303-388-2337, mountainsunpub.com

18 Cheesman Park:
From Graveyard to Gardens

BOUNDARIES: 12th Ave., Humboldt St., 8th Ave., York St., 11th Ave.
DISTANCE: 1.75 miles
DIFFICULTY: Easy
PARKING: Free parking along Humboldt St. and 12th Ave. and within Cheesman Park, as well as in the parking garage at Denver Botanic Gardens
PUBLIC TRANSIT: From downtown, take RTD route 10 bus to York St. in front of Denver Botanic Gardens; Denver B-cycle (denverbcycle.com) has a bicycle rental station in front of the gardens.

The first two blocks of this walk are along Denver's first designated residential historic district. The owners of these stately mansions sought the designation as more and more homes were replaced by the high-rise apartment buildings you will see in another part of this walk. Not only were exquisite homes demolished but the taller buildings also obliterated the mountain views from the individual homes. Despite the fact that Cheesman Park was the site of Denver's first cemetery, people saw the potential beauty of the area and began building some of these homes before there was actually a park next door. The eastern side of the old cemetery was converted to the Denver Botanic Gardens in 1958 and is worth walking around in any season to explore its indoor and outdoor gardens.

Note: Cars share the roads with pedestrians and cyclists within Cheesman Park.

Walk Description

Begin the walk at 12th Avenue and Humboldt Street and walk south on Humboldt Street. It does not matter which side of the street you choose to walk on as you admire the splendid historic homes and shady sidewalks. These next two blocks are also informally called "Humboldt Island" because of the concentration of preserved historic homes.

Cross 11th Avenue as you continue south on Humboldt Street. The house at 1075 Humboldt Street was built in 1906 and served as the governor's residence from 1922 to 1924 for then governor William Sweet. Presidents Teddy Roosevelt and William Howard Taft were guests and public speakers of the house at 1061 Humboldt Street when Harry Tammen, a cofounder of the *Denver Post,* resided here. The house at 1022 Humboldt Street was built with 46 rooms, including 9 bathrooms and a basement pool, in 1907.

Cross 10th Avenue and turn left to enter ❶ **Cheesman Park,** an 80-acre oasis in the middle of the city. Take a right on the gravel path and continue walking south. (There is a paved path for cyclists that at times runs parallel to this footpath.) Despite joggers, cyclists, and a road that cuts through the park, this stroll is fairly peaceful and often shady in summer. Cheesman Park is considered Capitol Hill's park as it's the largest in this neighborhood, and it's also associated with the local LGBT scene. The annual PrideFest typically begins here, and the parade route takes marchers/revelers to Civic Center Park (Walk 2).

The footpath will turn left and become parallel to 8th Avenue. Then it turns left again—giving you a glimpse into the backyards of some spectacular mansions—as you head north.

Cross 9th Avenue (there is no street sign at this intersection) and go right (the grass quickly turns into a sidewalk).

As you walk east on 9th Avenue, cross Race Street. The half blocks on your left dead-end into the ❷ **Denver Botanic Gardens,** and you can see the trees, flowers, and paths just beyond the fence and even hear birdsongs coming from deep within the lush setting.

Continue on 9th Avenue and cross Vine Street, then Gaylord Street. The homes and their yards on your left are so well kept that it is often hard to tell where the Denver Botanic Gardens

Flower gardens add to the beauty of the Cheesman Park Memorial Pavilion.

ends or begins. Don't be fooled! It is almost too good to be true: the "home" at 909 York Street is actually part of the gardens' administrative offices.

Turn left on York Street and walk north around the front entrance of the 24-acre Denver Botanic Gardens. Inside the main gardens area on your left there is a gift shop, Offshoots Café, a tropical conservatory, ponds, fountains, native plant gardens, rose gardens, a science pyramid, and much more. Across the street is not only the parking garage but also a children's garden that is partially on the garage roof. Although there is a fee to enter the gardens, you can see some plantings and sculpture as you walk the perimeter for free.

At 11th Avenue turn left again. Walk west back toward Cheesman Park. While there are some historic homes on this stretch, it seems a world away from the mansions on the south side of the gardens with the many high-rise apartment buildings on this north side.

Cross Gaylord Street, then Vine Street and Race Street, and continue west on 11th Avenue until the sidewalk ends and the grass of Cheesman Park takes over the sidewalk.

Go left on the gravel footpath briefly, then right on the asphalt path and cross another paved path. As the path merges with the formal gardens of the ❸ **Cheesman Park Memorial Pavilion,** feel free to walk about in any direction. Stop and smell the roses—literally! During Denver's own City Beautiful movement, then Mayor Robert Speer asked for private bidders to make an offer on building a memorial in the park. Alice Cheesman had this neoclassical pavilion

Backstory: Once a Graveyard . . .

Due to a series of unfortunate events, some of the bodies buried in Denver's first cemetery remain here despite its transformation to a popular park and gardens many, many years ago. Sometime in the 1870s, City Cemetery became such a forlorn wasteland that no one would pay to be buried there and instead chose the newer and grander Riverside and Fairmount Cemeteries on the outskirts of town (see Walks 12 and 31, respectively). As City Cemetery slid into its decline, many graves were left unmarked or vandalized. When it came time to remove the bodies, political scandal ended the official work of moving the remains elsewhere and citizens were given 90 days to find and move their own relatives' corpses. Who or what was left behind remains there still. During the 2008 renovation of the Denver Botanic Gardens, caskets and bones were unearthed from those bygone cemetery days.

of Colorado Yule marble built with formal gardens, fountains, and a reflecting pond in honor of her deceased husband, Walter Cheesman. Her donation was large enough to also have the park renamed for the family.

Walk through the pavilion and you'll see the panoramic mountain views to the west that make this such a popular place for family and wedding photographs. Be aware that the west side steps out of the pavilion are on either side of the flowerbed in the center. On the west side is a MOUNTAIN INDEX plaque with elevation and location of 30 peaks that might be seen from this vantage point. (This is also a good time to get out your hat and sunscreen, as the remainder of the walk does not provide much tree shade.)

From the pavilion walk west and cross the road (look both ways as this is a road for cars) to reenter the park. At the T take a right and walk north, then take a left at the first spur.

Cross another road and turn left on the asphalt path as it nears the ❹ playground.

Kid Tip: If you aren't old enough to read this yourself, this could be the perfect playground for you! I always have loved those little bouncy animals you can ride in playgrounds.

Don't miss the historic sign on the right of the path that tells of some of the park's colorful past and about the people who were involved in making it into the park it is today.

Continue on the path as it swerves right and then left. Cross the asphalt bike path, then turn right on the gravel footpath and walk north.

Cross 11th Avenue and walk one more block to 12th Avenue. Turn left and return to the sidewalk. Walk one block to Humboldt Street to complete the loop. This walk can be combined with Walk 1 by walking west on 12th Avenue to Pennsylvania Street.

Cheesman Park

Point of Interest

1 Cheesman Park   Bound by 13th Ave., 8th Ave., High St., and Franklin St.

2 Denver Botanic Gardens   1005 York St., 720-865-3500, botanicgardens.org

3 Cheesman Park Memorial Pavilion

4 Cheesman Park playground

19 Cherry Creek North and Country Club Historic District: Make It a Day of Luxury

BOUNDARIES: Humboldt St., 1st Ave., Steele St., 5th Ave.
DISTANCE: 3.5 miles
DIFFICULTY: Easy
PARKING: Metered parking along Cherry Creek North streets; fee parking lot on Milwaukee St. between 1st and 2nd Aves.
PUBLIC TRANSIT: The RTD 1 and 2 buses make stops on 1st Ave.; Denver B-cycle (denverbcycle.com) has stations in Cherry Creek North.

The Cherry Creek North shopping and dining area has long been associated with wealth, and it is no accident that it is easy walking distance from one of Denver's toniest neighborhoods, the Country Club Historic District adjacent to the exclusive Denver Country Club. This walk could— and maybe should—be broken into two separate walks with a long lunch in the middle. Start with window-shopping just a portion of this 16-block district of hundreds of boutiques, restaurants, and galleries before choosing a place for lunch. Then cross over to see a 1920s castle and other grand homes in the Denver Country Club neighborhood and return for some more serious shopping, another nibble at a café, or it might be time for a drink by then.

Walk Description

Begin this walk where Fillmore Street meets 2nd Avenue and there is a mix of shops and eateries. One of my favorite places for lunch in Denver is right here—**❶ Pasta Pasta Pasta,** a simple and always very good Italian restaurant with a selection of more than pasta each day. Keep in mind that I have not listed every shop, art gallery, and restaurant, but just some of my favorites. Hopefully you can enjoy making discoveries of your own here.

This area is named for Cherry Creek, which is south of here and runs downstream to Confluence Park (see Walk 7).

Walk north on Fillmore Street. The **❷ Hermitage Antiquarian Bookshop**—down below street level—with its rare books and comfy spots for leisurely research and browsing is worth a look.

Turn left on 3rd Avenue. Another wonderful place for a meal is **❸ Crêpes 'n Crêpes,** with every kind of sweet or savory crêpe you can imagine on their menu. If the weather is warm, try their bright little patio. At the intersection of 3rd Avenue and Detroit Street is the **❹ Artisan Center,** a go to for home, jewelry, and children's gifts. It is also packed during the holidays.

Turn left on Detroit Street. Tucked back a little from the street is **❺ MAX,** Denver's premier women's fashion shop for those who prefer Stella McCartney, Helmut Lang, Prada, and other big-name designers. Across the street is **❻ Garbarini,** where local gals go for Donald Pliner or Barbara Bui shoes, Nicole Miller or Robert Rodriguez collections, and just-right jeans.

Turn right on 2nd Avenue. To your left is **❼ Hapa Sushi,** perfect for a lunch, dinner, or happy hour sushi fix.

Turn right on Clayton Street. Looking across 2nd Avenue you will see the **❽ Cherry Cricket,** a local institution for burgers—especially green chile burgers—since 1950. It's a throwback to a time when this neighborhood was less upscale.

Walking north on Clayton Street you will see the **❾ Show of Hands Gallery** on the right, which features Colorado artists and handmade objects. Note as you cross 3rd Avenue, to the left closer to Columbine Street is **❿ Revampt,** a boutique of recycled goods turned into home furnishings (perfect for dad/husband/other men's gifts, I've found).

The Cherry Cricket has been a local institution since 1950.

After crossing 3rd Avenue, the shops of Cherry Creek North fall away, and it becomes a residential neighborhood. Once this area was mostly made up of small bungalows, but those are quite rare now, and you will see it is almost entirely newly built townhomes through here.

Turn left on 4th Avenue and walk west. At James N. Manley Park, follow the slightly winding path on the park's southern edge to Josephine Street and cross the street.

Walk one block west to York Street and cross the street. For this portion of the walk through the Country Club Historic District there will be several blocks without sidewalks, and you will be walking in the street at times. This area was designed by Denver's landscape architect Saco DeBoer, who had a hand in other parts of the greater neighborhood on this walk.

Turn right on Circle Drive and walk north. On your left at 475 Circle Drive is a castle that Mary Dean Reed had built between 1926 and 1931. Reed's husband made a fortune in real estate, ranching, oil, and mining before he died and left her millions. (For more information on Mary Reed and her daughter, see Walk 23.) In her book *Country Club Heritage: A History and Guide to a Denver Neighborhood,* Alice Millett Bakemeier writes that details in the house included "dwarfs doing various tasks" carved into the red oak paneling of a library balcony, Italian hand-carved marble fireplaces, bronze plaques depicting the seasons, and many more fantastic designs. The house at 505 Circle Drive was also commissioned by Mrs. Reed for her sister to live in.

Follow the road as it curves left and you begin walking south on Race Street. Bakemeier writes that the house at 545 Circle Drive was designed by architect Burnham Hoyt in 1941, who designed the Red Rocks Amphitheatre (see Walk 27). The house at 515 Race Street was also designed by Burnham Hoyt and in 1999 was donated to the University of Denver as a residence for the chancellor, then later sold (see Walk 23).

Turn right on 5th Avenue when the circle ends and walk west to Williams Street.

Turn left on Williams Street and walk to 4th Avenue. Williams Street curves right and merges into 4th Avenue.

Turn right on 4th Avenue and walk west. At Franklin Street you will see the original entry archway for the Denver Country Club. Bakemeier writes that the group of realtors developing the country club and golf course hired architect William Ellsworth Fisher, "who designed the distinctive Spanish entrance gates at Franklin, Gilpin, and High Streets along 4th Avenue. "To leave room for the large estates, 2nd Avenue and Williams Street were not platted. In fact, houses had to cost a minimum amount: "On certain quarters deeds will not be given to the ground without the insertion of a condition that a home costing not less than $10,000 be built." The minimum ranged depending on the exact block.

At Humboldt Street turn left. This area was developed as the Park Club Place subdivision before the country club. To your right at 375 Humboldt Street is another, but altogether different, house designed by architects Merrill and Burnham Hoyt in 1922. Occasionally the Hoyt brothers worked together, sometimes separately. Merrill Hoyt designed the Georgian Revival house at 369 Humboldt Street, writes Bakemeier. On the corner of 3rd Avenue and Humboldt Street is the house that former Mayor Robert J. Speer had built in 1911 and lived in until his death in 1918 while he was still mayor.

Turn left on 3rd Avenue and walk east. Reading Bakemeier's book gives a glimpse into the families who have owned and lived in these great homes—the presidents of oil companies, realtors, bankers, politicians—and also how few owners many of the homes have had in the past 100 or so years. While you might see the occasional fellow pedestrian or bicycler on these quiet streets, it's more likely it will be so peaceful that you can hear the sound of a single leaf drop. Impressive, considering you are only two blocks away from the six lanes of cars and buses on busy Speer Boulevard.

Turn right on Gilpin Street and walk south. Only three streets have the wide center parkways, the vision of Mayor Speer to have the city parks continuously connected by grassy, tree-lined strips like this. You are within sight of the Denver Country Club, whose entrance is directly across Speer Boulevard (also called 1st Avenue from here east). The club was founded in 1887, and club members bought a wheat farm in 1902 to turn it into a civilized place for sporting events such as golf and polo on 240 acres with secured water rights.

Cherry Creek runs down the middle of Speer Boulevard, then disappears for a bit and reappears on the east side of the country club. Speer Boulevard was once called the Cherokee Trail when it was a footpath for Native Americans, according to Bakemeier, then it became a trail for prospective miners headed to the mountains. Quiet little Cherry Creek used to flood the area, and as development increased and a 1912 flood wiped out the club's golf course before a tournament, it was dammed and diverted.

Turn left at the last crossover in the center parkway and walk north on Gilpin Street. The houses at 385 and 380 Gilpin Street were designed by Burnham Hoyt and Merrill and Burnham Hoyt in 1925 and 1926.

Turn right on 4th Avenue to walk east. The trolley cars used to run along 4th Avenue too.

Turn right on Race Court and walk south until the street ends.

Curve left with the road as it becomes 3rd Avenue and you walk north back into the shops and restaurants of Cherry Creek North.

At the corner of Josephine Street and 3rd Avenue is **⓫ Little Ollie's,** where businesspeople and families pop in for large portions of Chinese food for lunch or dinner. You walk past some of the previously mentioned businesses, such as Revampt and the Artisan Center.

Next up is a bit of whimsical public art across the street from the Ross Cherry Creek Library: the sculpture *Sip n' Splash* by artist James Haire. It's a reminder that Cherry Creek North is home to one of the country's premier annual art festivals each July 4 weekend. The streets of Cherry Creek North are closed and filled with artists' booths, stages for concerts, and food vendors. If you're not with the kids, check out **⓬ Le Soutien,** a women's lingerie store with the ultimate in customer service.

Down the street along 3rd Avenue is **⓭ Cucina Colore,** for contemporary Italian cuisine and award-winning wines.

Turn right on Steele Street. About midblock on the right side is the **⓮ Lawrence Covell** store, with designers like Jil Sander, Rag & Bone, and Etro for both men and women.

Turn right on 2nd Avenue to walk back to Fillmore Street and end the walk.

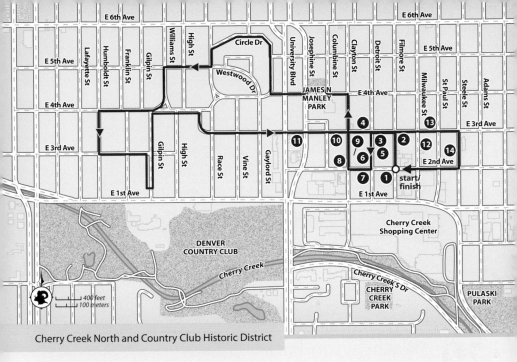

Cherry Creek North and Country Club Historic District

Points of Interest

1. **Pasta Pasta Pasta** 278 Fillmore St., 303-377-2782

2. **The Hermitage Antiquarian Bookshop** 290 Fillmore St., 303-388-6811, hermitagebooks.com

3. **Crêpes 'n Crêpes** 2816 E. 3rd Ave., 303-320-4184, crepesncrepes.net

4. **The Artisan Center** 2757 E. 3rd Ave., 303-333-1201, artisancenterdenver.com

5. **MAX** 264 Detroit St., 303-321-4949, maxclothing.com

6. **Garbarini** 239 Detroit St., 303-333-8686, garbarinishop.com

7. **Hapa Sushi** 2780 E. 2nd Ave., 303-322-9554, hapasushi.com

8. **Cherry Cricket** 2641 E. 2nd Ave., 303-322-7666, cherrycricket.com

9. **Show of Hands Gallery** 210 Clayton St., 303-399-0201, showofhandsdenver.com

10. **Revampt** 2601 E. 3rd Ave., 720-536-5464, revamptgoods.com

11. **Little Ollie's** 2364 E. 3rd Ave., 303-316-8888, littleolliescherrycreek.com

12. **Le Soutien** 246 Milwaukee St., 303-377-0515, lesoutien.com

13. **Cucina Colore** 3041 E. 3rd Ave., 303-393-6917, cucinacolore.com

14. **Lawrence Covell** 225 Steele St., 303-320-1023, lawrencecovell.com

20 Washington Park:
Run, Walk, Play Here

Above: Mount Vernon Garden hugs the edge of Grasmere Lake in Washington Park.

BOUNDARIES: E. Virginia Ave., S. University Blvd., E. Mississippi Ave., S. Downing St.
DISTANCE: 3 miles
DIFFICULTY: Easy
PARKING: Free parking lots on Downing St. side; parking on roads within the park or side streets outside of park is free.
PUBLIC TRANSIT: The RTD 12 bus makes stops on Downing St. on Washington Park's west side; RTD light-rail H, E, and F lines all stop at Louisiana/Pearl west of Washington Park.

Busy. That's the first word that comes to mind when I think of how to describe Washington Park. Big. That's the next word that comes to mind for this 165-acre park just south of downtown Denver. It is certainly a lively place with room for almost every kind of recreation you can think of, during any time of year. Locals call it Wash Park, and it is probably Denver's most popular park given all the amenities in one place with two big lakes, a pond (fishing allowed in all of them), flower gardens, multiuse trails, boat rentals, benches and picnic areas, tennis courts, a large grassy meadow, trees for shade and brilliant fall color, mountain views, historic buildings—and it is all easy walking distance from some very good restaurants and shops.

Note: Cars share the roads with pedestrians and cyclists within the park. Washington Park is officially open daily, 6 a.m.–11 p.m.

Walk Description

Begin at the park's original entrance on the north side where Marion Street Parkway and Virginia Avenue intersect. More than once I have driven up to ❶ **Washington Park** on a sunny weekend and, when seeing the many joggers going by, thought to myself, "Uh-oh! There must be a race today." But no, it's like that all of the time in this park. Rollerbladers, kids learning to ride their first bicycle, moms and dads pushing strollers, bicyclers, pedestrians in deep conversation or listening to music with their headphones, dogwalkers, and most of all, joggers, fill the many roads and trails in Washington Park. As you walk you will mostly hear the slight scrape of running shoes against the pavement or gravel, along with people talking and laughing as they play and exercise here.

Facing the ❷ **Dos Chappell Bathhouse,** walk around the right side of the building, using the pedestrian lane of the road. The Craftsman-style bathhouse opened in 1911 and served as changing rooms for swimmers in Smith Lake in summer, then as a warming house for ice skaters in winter. Once swimming and ice-skating were no longer allowed on the lake after 1957, the bathhouse fell into disrepair for many years until a renovation in the 1990s when it became offices for the Volunteers for Outdoor Colorado. It is now named after VOC's founder, Dos Chappell.

Veer left to join a footpath behind the bathhouse that circles the lake, and continue walking south. From here you get the sense of the wide-open space of this park as you look left over 16-acre ❸ **Smith Lake.** The lake is named for John W. Smith, who created not only the lake (a natural depression that may have been a buffalo wallows) but also a ditch that runs through the park, historically called Smith's Ditch and now renamed City Ditch. Completed in 1867, the ditch made it possible for water from the South Platte River to be diverted about 25 miles downstream to Capitol Hill and changed the arid plains to a lush and hospitable place to grow the city. Today the water for City Ditch comes from a different source than the South Platte River.

On the lake's south side is the boathouse and pavilion, built in 1913 and designed by architect J. J. B. Benedict (see Walk 25) and restored in the 1980s. Today, boat and bicycle rentals are made from a booth next to the boathouse, and you might be able to see Long's Peak to the northwest and Mount Evans to the west from the boathouse.

Washington Park features two scenic lakes.

Stay on this path as it curves around small white park maintenance buildings.

Kid Tip: If the boats and bikes aren't out when you are doing this walk, then just across from the boathouse is a huge playground that I think is just as fun as the bikes and boats.

As you begin to walk toward the ❹ **Washington Park Recreation Center** (an indoor pool means that there is still swimming allowed at Washington Park, just not in the lakes), stop at the large sign with historical photos and details about the park's founding.

Turn around and walk briefly north again before the path curves left.

Cross the road as you turn left and walk into the flower garden. In a mild year, there is a very good chance you will see flowers still blooming in fuchsia, violet, gold, and all the colors of the rainbow into October. It's a little bit quieter in this flower garden since runners stay on the main artery roads.

Turn left and walk south through the flower garden.

Turn left and cross the road as you leave the flower garden behind.

Go right on the paved path to walk south along the park's Great Meadow. This area is a combination adult and child play area where volleyball nets are set up and people are playing Frisbee and soccer—all at once—on this huge grassy field not crossed by the park's many trails.

Turn right and cross the road toward ❺ **Grasmere Lake** at the second playground.

Kid Tip: During the walk toward the second—and smaller—playground, I like to climb the trees and watch/feed the ducks in the lakes.

This man-made lake on the park's south end is named for England's own lake of the same name and town where poet William Wordsworth lived. Wordsworth was one of the Lake Poets, known for their English Romantic style, and the hope in designing this park was that it might inspire "literary and artistic achievements."

Turn left after you cross Smith's Ditch to walk east with the lake on your right and the ditch on your left.

Turn left between the hedges of Mount Vernon Garden, modeled on Martha Washington's Mount Vernon Upper Garden. This small formal garden is also off the beaten path from joggers and cyclists.

Turn right to walk on the road or cross the road and join the footpath again as you head east out of the park. Yes, you can explore the entire park and there is more, but this walk exits here for a miniurban detour . . . or maybe just lunch, if you didn't bring a picnic.

Cross S. Franklin Street as you begin walking east on Mississippi Avenue (the road leading out of the park). The bungalows of Washington Park were primarily built in the 1920s and 1930s during a building boom for this area that used to be the town of South Denver. As you walk on these side streets on a weekend with mild sunny weather, chances are good you'll see more pedestrians than cars along your way.

Turn left on S. Gaylord Street, Washington Park's hub of restaurants and shops. Old South Gaylord Street bills itself as the second-oldest shopping district in Denver. Before you head down the block, make a note of two restaurants across the street—❻ **Washington Park Grille**, a neighborhood favorite for contemporary Italian food for lunch or dinner, and ❼ **Devil's Food Bakery & Cookery** for fresh baked goods and savory meals for breakfast, lunch, and dinner.

On the west side of the street is ❽ **Wish Boutique** for women, ❾ **Trout's American Sportswear** for men, and ❿ **Sports Plus** for gently used and gently priced sporting goods for the whole family, as well as art galleries and other shops.

On the east side are more restaurants: ⓫ **The Tavern Wash Park** with a busy bar and American classics like burgers, Philly cheese steak sandwiches, and salads; and ⓬ **Homegrown Tap & Dough**, which uses locally sourced ingredients for pizzas, burgers, pastas, and more. There are additional restaurants here to try depending on the time of day, whom you are with, and what you crave.

Continue walking north on S. Gaylord Street as it returns to residential blocks only.

Turn right on Ohio Avenue to walk two blocks to University Boulevard.

Kid Tip: Even if you're excited to get back to the park, this next stop is worth the time. If you follow the instructions below, you'll end up at Bonnie Brae Ice Cream—my second-favorite place for ice cream in Denver.

Turn left and cross Ohio Avenue. You are on the outer edge of the Bonnie Brae neighborhood with two eponymous places to try: ⓭ **Bonnie Brae Ice Cream** and ⓮ **Bonnie Brae Tavern**, both longtime Denver institutions for this neighborhood. On hot days, there is a line out the door for Bonnie Brae Ice Cream, and the tavern has pizza often declared the best in Denver. On the opposite corner you will see the ⓕ **Eugene Field Branch Library,** named for the popular children's author (more on his Denver connection coming up).

Turn around and walk west on Ohio Avenue about eight blocks back to Washington Park. Just before turning right into the park, you will see some white buildings on the left. These are the Whitehead Brothers Farmstead buildings from 1892 when the park was mainly their farm. Since then they've served as housing for park superintendents and are now used for park maintenance facilities.

Walk north on the path to the ⓖ **Eugene Field Cottage.** Field came to Denver in 1881 to work as managing editor for the *Denver Tribune* and lived in this little house when it was located on W. Colfax Avenue across from the U.S. Mint at Denver (see Walk 2). Field spent only two years in Denver but was well loved for his children's poems, such as "Little Boy Blue" and "Wynken, Blynken, and Nod," by the time Molly Brown (whose own historic home can be seen on Walk 1) stepped in to save his home from demolition in the 1920s. It was moved to Washington Park and turned into a branch library, then closed to the public when the new one opened on University Boulevard in 1970. It is not open to the public and is used for civic organizations.

Follow the path as it curves around Eugene Field Cottage and you will see the "Wynken, Blynken, and Nod" statue on the other side that evokes the characters from Field's well-known children's rhyme.

Turn left to cross the road and join the path as it curves around Smith Lake to the right. As the path curves left and west around Smith Lake, peek over to the right to see Lily Pond, a fishing hole for kids only.

Take the right fork when the path divides. This will take you back to the starting point in front of Dos Chappell Bathhouse and the end of the loop.

Points of Interest

① **Washington Park** S. Downing St. and E. Louisiana Ave., 303-698-4962

② **Dos Chappell Bathhouse** 600 S. Marion Pkwy.

③ **Smith Lake**

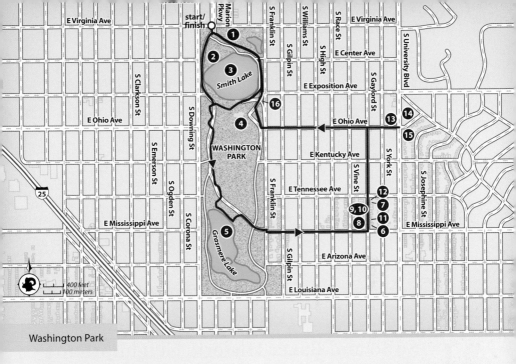

Washington Park

④ Washington Park Recreation Center 701 S. Franklin St., 720-865-3400, denvergov.org

⑤ Grasmere Lake

⑥ Washington Park Grille 1096 S. Gaylord St., 303-777-0707, washparkgrille.com

⑦ Devil's Food Bakery 1020 S. Gaylord St., 303-733-7448, devilsfooddenver.com

⑧ Wish Boutique 1071 S. Gaylord St., 303-733-4848, wishdenver.com

⑨ Trout's American Sportswear 1077 S. Gaylord St., 303-733-3983, trouts.net

⑩ Sports Plus 1055 S. Gaylord St., 303-777-6613, sportsplusdenver.com

⑪ The Tavern Wash Park 1066 S. Gaylord St., 303-733-0350, tavernhg.com/wash_park

⑫ Homegrown Tap & Dough 1001 S. Gaylord St., 720-459-8736, tapanddough.com

⑬ Bonnie Brae Ice Cream 799 S. University Blvd., 303-777-0808, bonniebraeicecream.com

⑭ Bonnie Brae Tavern 740 S. University Blvd., 303-777-2262, bonniebraetavern.com

⑮ Eugene Field Branch Library 810 S. University Blvd., 720-865-0240, denverlibrary.org

⑯ Eugene Field Cottage 715 S. Franklin St.

21 SoBo and Baker Historic Neighborhood:
Victorian Homes Meet Trendy Shops and Restaurants

Above: The Mayan Theatre on South Broadway has unique architectural details inside and out.

BOUNDARIES: 3rd Ave., Bannock St., Lincoln St., E. Bayaud Ave.
DISTANCE: 1.25 miles
DIFFICULTY: Easy
PARKING: Free parking is available on side streets; metered parking is along Broadway.
PUBLIC TRANSIT: RTD 0 bus makes stops along S. Broadway.

Denver's South Broadway business district, most recently dubbed SoBo, was once called Miracle Mile, for how the strip reinvented itself as a commercial hub in the early 1900s. Before that the street was lined with small markets and mansions that were then demolished to make room for multistory buildings that housed department stores, hotels, apartments, and restaurants, all easily reached by the cable cars that had replaced horse transportation and ran down the street. As the area slid into decline in the 1970s, another wave of "renewal" threatened the historic buildings, such as the Mayan Theatre, but in the 1980s the surrounding neighborhood of Victorian homes was designated the Baker Historic District, and landmark status was given to other important structures. Businesses began to resettle the area, and it has been rediscovered all over again. Today's SoBo is a draw for 20-something hipsters with their brand of cool reflected in the shops, restaurants, bars, and nightclubs. Beyond that audience, there are sophisticated art galleries, independent cinema, and swanky dining options for any age and interest.

Walk Description

This walk begins at ❶ **St. Augustine Orthodox Christian Church** at the corner of 3rd Avenue and Acoma Street. St. Augustine was built in 1912 as St. John's Evangelical Church for a German Lutheran congregation. A parochial school affiliated with that church was destroyed in the 1960s. St. Augustine is proud of their choir, which sings Gregorian chanting as part of the liturgy.

Cross Acoma Street and walk west one block to Bannock Street. This is part of the Baker Historic District Neighborhood, recognized since 1985, and the little pockets like this that you will see on this walk show off what is the largest number of middle-class Queen Anne–style homes in Denver, primarily built from the mid 1880s to 1893. William and Elizabeth Byers homesteaded much of the Baker neighborhood. William Byers began printing the *Rocky Mountain News* in 1859 (the newspaper was folded in 2009, just shy of its 150th birthday). While two mayors lived in this neighborhood, many of the residents were teachers, butchers, railroad workers, and other businessmen. The houses at 144 and 140 3rd Avenue are classic Queen Anne with the addition of round towers in front of each.

Turn left at Bannock Street and cross 3rd Avenue to walk one block south to 2nd Avenue. The house at 233 Bannock Street is a good example of the Denver Square architectural style that was favored after the Queen Anne style was less popular.

Turn left on 2nd Avenue. On the right side of the street is the ❷ **Episcopal Church of St. Peter and St. Mary,** built in 1891 and reminiscent of Cornish churches in England. Architect Charles H. Lee also designed the Elitch Gardens' Theater, which is all that is left standing in the former amusement park of the Highlands neighborhood (see Walk 11).

Turn right at Acoma Street and cross 2nd Avenue.

Turn left and cross Acoma Street to walk east on 2nd Avenue. On your right will be ❸ **Denver Firehouse Station No 11,** built in 1936 in the Art Deco style.

Cross Broadway and turn right to walk south. The one-of-a-kind ❹ **Mayan Theatre** is on your left. The Mayan replaced a damaged theatre (the Queen Theatre, originally built in 1911 as the Rex Theatre) and was designed by architect Montana Fallis in 1930. The theatre is ornately decorated inside and out with Mayan Indian images. The theatre was saved from demolition in 1984 and refurbished into a three-screen movie house as part of Landmark Theatres, showing alternative, foreign, and independent films.

Cross First Avenue and looking west notice ❺ **Señor Burrito,** a little hole in the wall that makes an excellent smothered burrito for lunch or budget premovie meal. On the corner is ❻ **The Hornet,** a large bar and restaurant with a lunch and dinner menu that will have something for any taste. A couple of doors down is ❼ **Sweet Action Ice Cream,** known for their locally sourced ingredients and mind-boggling flavors, such as baklava, salted butterscotch, Stranahan's Whiskey Brickle, and vegan varieties too. Sweet Action is open late for cravings too.

It's True Love for affordable shoes here.
photographed by Evan Semon/Visit Denver

Now it's time to shop a little. ❽ **True Love Shoes** sells women's boots, high heels, handbags, jewelry, and other accessories. Starlet (see Walk 9 for another outpost) is a feminine mix of accessories and vintage finds. If you like vintage, head directly to ❾ **Boss Unlimited** for vintage and costume clothing for the whole family; ❿ **Fancy Tiger** is an urban hipster's dream of crafts, and classes to become crafty, along with some locally made items; ⓫ **Sewn** is for the not-crafty person who just appreciates homemade and locally made and . . . eclectic style; ⓬ **Hazel & Dewey** has housewares for the urban kitchen. My perennial favorite for shopping here remains ⓭ **Decade,** a delightful mix of toiletries, clothing, jewelry, books, and other little things you didn't know you needed but now must have.

Speaking of kitchens and being hip, ⓮ **Beatrice & Woodsley** not only serves up delicious brunch and dinner menus, paired with wine and champagne lists, but also a tea service with scones, cucumber sandwiches, and sweets in a very cool, yes, woodsy, décor.

Added to the mix of great little restaurants and shops are some nightclubs, including 3 Kings Tavern, for those who like their rock music loud and intense with a good pool game for distraction, and Hi-Dive, a grunge live music club. You'll also find Sputnik, a diner for those late-night snacks or "hangover brunch" on weekends.

Artists have also colonized here with the Gildar Gallery, displaying very modern sculpture and paintings; then at the corner of Bayaud Avenue, look to the right and west down Bayaud Avenue to see Open Press Ltd., a fine art printmaking facility and gallery that features local and national artists. They also offer printmaking workshops.

Turn left at Bayaud Avenue and walk east one block to Lincoln Street. On the corner is the Ross-Broadway Branch Library, a tiny yet oh-so-cool Modernist building designed by architect Victor Hornbein in 1951.

Turn left on Lincoln Street and walk north to Ellsworth Avenue. Cross Ellsworth Avenue to stand in front of the ⑮ **South Broadway Christian Church.** Interesting history and architecture accompany this medieval castle of a church. A heartbroken John Sutton convinced the retiring pastor from his church to stay in Colorado to help create a new church in honor of Sutton's deceased wife. With Sutton's generous funding, the first cornerstone of rhyolite from Castle Rock, Colorado, was placed in 1891 with Mrs. Sutton's bible beneath it. When Mr. Sutton had given all his money to the church, he asked to live in two rooms in the church tower where he lived until 1901 at the age of 81. Stained glass inside the church also honors the Suttons.

Turn left to walk west on Ellsworth Avenue. On the right is Dougherty's, where the specialty is stuffed burgers as well as shepherd's pie and other Irish favorites for lunch and dinner.

Continue walking west on Ellsworth Avenue to Dailey Park. The next several blocks take you back into the Baker Historic District for a pleasant stroll by many restored Queen Anne cottages. What makes the Queen Anne architectural style so precious is individual details put into the woodwork—flowers, sunbursts, birds, and other ornamentation—now highlighted by bright paint colors in the best of these homes. This style also favored wraparound porches, particularly on corner lots.

Turn right on Cherokee Street to walk to Irvington Place.

Turn right on Irvington Place and walk east to Broadway. With mature trees and flower gardens, these blocks can be a surprisingly peaceful walk so close to the cars and buses on Broadway. Back in the 1880s and 1890s, many homes were also built on Broadway, but very few of those remain today. The last block dead-ends into a small cul-de-sac at Broadway.

Turn left on Broadway and walk north to 3rd Avenue. There are a few more recommended places if you want to go beyond 3rd Avenue by a couple of blocks. Wizard's Chest is our go-to toy store in Denver, and practically next door is Meininger's, a classic art supply store that is also a great gift shop. Across the street is Metropolitan Frame Company, which is also an art gallery.

Or, go back where you started and turn left on 3rd Avenue and walk one block to Acoma Street. Turn right to cross 3rd Avenue and return to St. Augustine Orthodox Christian Church.

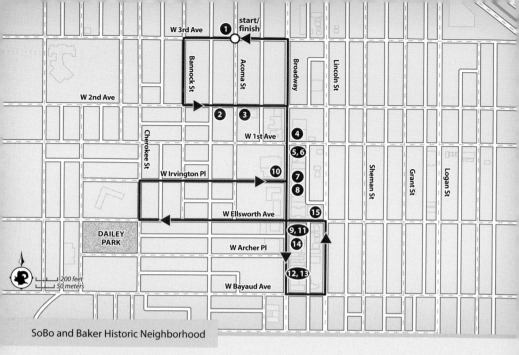

SoBo and Baker Historic Neighborhood

Points of Interest

1 St. Augustine Orthodox Christian Church 55 W. 3rd Ave., 303-698-2433, staugustinedenver.org

2 Episcopal Church of St. Peter and St. Mary 126 W. 2nd Ave., 303-722-8781, stspeterandmary.org

3 Denver Firehouse Station No 11 40 W. 2nd Ave.

4 Mayan Theatre 110 Broadway, 303-744-6799, landmarktheatres.com

5 Señor Burrito 12 E. 1st Ave., 303-733-0747

6 The Hornet 76 Broadway, 303-777-7676, hornetrestaurant.com

7 Sweet Action Ice Cream 52 Broadway, 303-282-4645, sweetactionicecream.com

8 True Love Shoes & Accessories 42 Broadway, 303-860-8783, trueloveshoes.com

9 Boss Unlimited 10 S. Broadway, 303-871-0373, bossvintage.com

10 Fancy Tiger 59 Broadway, 303-733-3855, fancytiger.com

11 Sewn 18 S. Broadway, 303-832-1493, sewndenver.com

12 Hazel & Dewey 70 S. Broadway, 303-777-1500, hazel-dewey.myshopify.com

13 Decade 56 S. Broadway, 303-733-2288, facebook.com/decadedenver

14 Beatrice & Woodsley 38 S. Broadway, 303-777-3505, beatriceandwoodsley.com

15 South Broadway Christian Church 23 Lincoln St., 303-722-4679, southbroadway.org

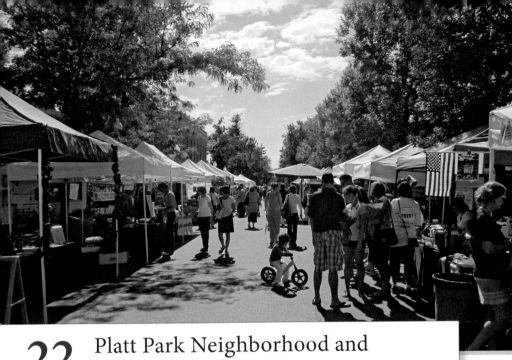

22 Platt Park Neighborhood and South Pearl Street: Step off the Light-Rail for Shopping and Dining in South Denver

Above: Crowds fill Old South Pearl Street during a weekly farmers market.

BOUNDARIES: E. Louisiana Ave., S. Pearl St., E. Iowa Ave., S. Grant St.
DISTANCE: Approx. 1.5 miles
DIFFICULTY: Easy
PARKING: Free on-street parking is available.
PUBLIC TRANSIT: RTD light-rail lines E, F, and H also stop at the Louisiana/Pearl depot, just a couple of blocks from the start/end of the walk.

The Platt Park neighborhood was originally part of the town of South Denver and an extension of the University of Denver community to the south of this area. After annexation with the city of Denver, spreading tramway car service made the neighborhood more accessible and appealing. In the 1950s I-25 cut the neighborhood's main commercial district, Old South Pearl Street, in half, and it struggled to survive. This walk takes you through the most vibrant few blocks of Old South Pearl Street, where a mass-transit line, the light-rail train, has once again brought new life to the area. On Sundays in summer and fall, one block of the street is closed for a bustling farmers market, and year-round many of the shops and restaurants emphasize locally grown ingredients, locally made items, and supporting locally owned businesses. A couple of blocks away is a historic park with its own unique story.

Walk Description

Begin the walk at the intersection of E. Louisiana Avenue and S. Pearl Street. On the southeast corner is ❶ The Village Cork, a small bistro featuring an ever-changing menu to match seasonally available produce paired with boutique wines. Directly across the street is ❷ Duffeyroll, legendary for their cinnamon buns, and also serving sandwiches, soups, and salads.

Walk south on S. Pearl Street. The businesses are mixed in with the residences in the first block or so of this walk. Check the calendar of events at southpearlstreet.com to find out about concerts, First Friday artwalks, and annual festivals.

Stop for a bite to eat along South Pearl Street.

On your right is ❸ Kaos Pizzeria, where they grow some of their own produce for their pizza toppings. On the left will be ❹ Stella's Coffeehaus, which kind of looks and feels like one of the actual houses on this street. On the right is ❺ Sushi Den, often named Denver's very best sushi restaurant—not just by local publications, but by my sushi-loving friends too! Next door, ❻ Izakaya Den is an offshoot of Sushi Den with a different ambience but just as good.

Cross Florida Avenue to stroll from shop to shop. ❼ Melrose & Madison has everything a girl needs to outfit for the next music festival in ruffles, lace, jumpsuits, and denim. ❽ 5 Green Boxes—twice! The midblock store is their home décor shop (think perfect girlfriend gifts), and the corner location is clothing and accessories (also makes a girlfriend happy). Check out the western wildlife and landscape paintings at ❾ Bell Studio Gallery. ❿ Yardbird (formerly Gaia Bistro in the former Black Pearl restaurant) is like a fancy diner with breakfast all day and a separate dinner menu featuring items like pot pies and other comfort foods. ⓫ **Uno Mas Taqueria** is a cousin to Kaos Pizzeria, with farm-fresh ingredients combined to make succulent tacos.

At the corner of Pearl Street and Iowa Avenue is ⓬ **Cameron United Methodist Church,** which was built between 1909 and 1913 in the Romanesque and Gothic Revival styles. The stained glass windows in the church were made and installed by the Watkins Stained Glass Studio, which has been in business in the Denver area since 1868. Their work can be seen in many Colorado churches and other buildings, including the Fairmount Mausoleum (see Walk 31). Today the church is also a community center for this neighborhood.

If you were to continue walking south, you would find a smattering of shops and restaurants for the next couple blocks.

If you want to stick to this route, turn right on E. Iowa Avenue to walk west two blocks to S. Logan Street.

Cross S. Logan Street to ⓭ **Platt Park** and walk on the park's southern perimeter for one block to S. Grant Street. Platt Park was named for Colonel James H. Platt, founder of the Platt Paper Company. Col. Platt is buried at Fairmount Cemetery (see Walk 31).

There is a little playground in the park with a merry-go-round and swings for the kiddos.

Turn right to walk north on S. Grant Street. The stone house on the right within Platt Park was built for James Fleming in 1892, and he served as the only mayor of what was once the town of South Denver. After Fleming sold the house in 1891, it served as the town hall, jail, and library before the town was annexed into the city of Denver.

Turn right on E. Florida Avenue and walk one block back to S. Logan Street. This 1913 branch library's full name is the ⓮ **Sarah Platt-Decker Branch Library.** Mrs. Platt-Decker was married to the above Col. Platt until his death in 1894 and then remarried Judge Westbrook S. Decker. She was a remarkable woman by all accounts and has been recognized by the Colorado Women's Hall of Fame. Among her many achievements, Mrs. Platt-Decker was the founder of the Denver Women's Club (Walk 1), a champion for equal rights for women, and was the first woman to serve on the board of pardons. "Three times a widow, she overcame personal grief for the nobler interest of humanity," states the biography on the Colorado Women's Hall of Fame website.

Cross S. Logan Street and walk two blocks back to S. Pearl Street.

Turn left and walk back to E. Louisiana Avenue to end the walk.

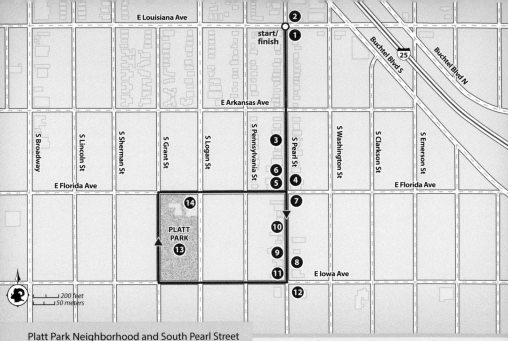

Platt Park Neighborhood and South Pearl Street

Points of Interest

1. The Village Cork 1300 S. Pearl St., 303-282-8399, villagecork.com

2. Duffeyroll Café 1290 S. Pearl St., 303-953-6890, duffeyrolls.com

3. Kaos Pizzeria 1439 S. Pearl St., 303-733-5267, kaospizzeria.com

4. Stella's Coffeehaus 1476 S. Pearl St., 303-777-1031, stellascoffee.com

5. Sushi Den 1487 S. Pearl St., 303-777-0826, sushiden.net

6. Izakaya Den 1487-A S. Pearl St., 303-777-0691, izakayaden.net

7. Melrose & Madison 1500 S. Pearl St., 303-777-7515, shopmelandmad.com

8. 5 Green Boxes 1596 S. Pearl St., 303-777-2331, 5greenboxes.com

9. Bell Studio Gallery 1573 S. Pearl St., 303-282-7343, susanbellfineart.com

10. Yardbird 1529 S. Pearl St., 303-777-0500, yardbirddenver.com

11. Uno Mas Taqueria 1585 S. Pearl St., 303-777-2866, unomastaqueria.com

12. Cameron United Methodist Church 1600 S. Pearl St., cameronchurch.org

13. Platt Park 1500 S. Grant St., denvergov.org

14. Sarah Platt-Decker Branch Library 1501 S. Logan St., 720-865-0220, denverlibrary.org

23 University of Denver Campus:
Stargazing and Alumni Stars

Above: The oldest, independent university in the Rocky Mountains

BOUNDARIES: S. Milwaukee St., E. Asbury Ave., S. Franklin St., E. Wesley Ave.
DISTANCE: Approx. 3 miles
DIFFICULTY: Easy
PARKING: Signs on Evans Ave. direct you to VISITOR PARKING lots; free on-street parking is around Observatory Park.
PUBLIC TRANSIT: The RTD light-rail F and H lines stop on the north end of the campus; Denver B-cycle (denverbcycle.com) has a station in front of the Driscoll Center; RTD 21, 24, and 79 buses all stop at the campus.

Founded in 1864 as the Colorado Seminary in downtown Denver, the University of Denver (DU) was relocated to a one-time potato farm in South Denver in the late 1880s. From these humble roots, it became the first and oldest independent university in the Rocky Mountain region. It seemed to start with visionaries and continue with them—first founder John Evans, who didn't want people to have to go back East for their higher education, then others like astronomy professor Herbert A. Howe, who oversaw construction of the first building on this campus (the Chamberlin Observatory), and on to Josef Korbel, founder of the university's graduate school of international studies and father of the first female United States secretary of state, Madeleine Albright. It's a who's who on the alumni list, with one of Korbel's star pupils, Condoleeza Rice, the first African American woman to serve as US secretary of state, *New York Times* editor Andrew Rosenthal, Peter Coors of the Coors Brewing Company, former Secretary of the Interior Gale Norton, and many more. This walk takes you from the observatory through the campus arboretum, historic and modern buildings, and through a bit of the surrounding neighborhood.

Walk Description

Begin at the ❶ **Chamberlin Observatory** in Observatory Park east of the University of Denver campus, the corner of Warren Avenue and Fillmore Street. The Chamberlin Observatory was built between 1890 and 1894, driven by the vision of DU's first astronomy professor, Herbert Howe, and designed by architect Robert Roeschlaub. It was named for its benefactor, local business-man and amateur astronomer Humphrey Barker Chamberlin. The dome has a 20-inch aperture Clark-Saegmuller refracting telescope and is open for weekly public viewing.

Walk west on E. Warren Avenue. As you get closer to the campus, the splendid homes—both historic and new—make way for two-story apartment buildings and fraternity and sorority houses.

Cross S. University Boulevard and stay on the left side of the circular drive. To the left is the ❷ **Iliff School of Theology's** historic building, built in 1892. The school was started with a finan-cial gift from Elizabeth Iliff Warren (see Walk 31), widow of John Wesley Iliff, a very successful cattle rancher, and wife of Bishop Henry White Warren. The school was founded in 1889 as part of the University of Denver; it closed around 1900 and then reopened in 1910 as a separate entity from the university. Since the 1980s, the schools have had a joint graduate program.

Turn right as you come to the front of the ❸ **Mary Reed Building.** Mary Reed ran a realty company in the 1920s after her husband died and had a castle built for her private home near the Country Club neighborhood (see Walk 19). Reed's daughter, Margery Reed, was a DU alumna and assistant English professor who died at the age of 31. Mrs. Reed made many substantial gifts to the school in honor of her daughter. The Mary Reed Building was constructed as a library in 1932, and a portrait of her hangs in the Renaissance Room of the building, per her request. Today it is an administrative building and used for graduate studies programs.

DU's Chamberlin Observatory was the first building on campus.

Continue walking north as the sidewalk winds closer to the historic ❹ **University Hall,** the campus's first building, which opened in 1892. According to Steve Fisher in *University Park and South Denver,* it is called "Old Main" and originally housed everything from a chapel to classrooms and a gymnasium. Fisher notes that a multimillion-dollar renovation made it possible for the building to still be used today.

Straight ahead is the ❺ **Buchtel Memorial Tower**—or what's left of it. The chapel was completed in 1917 and named for the university's third chancellor, Henry A. Buchtel, who had also served as governor of Colorado. It was dedicated as the Memorial Chapel for the university alumni who died in World War I. There was a tower like the one you see before you on each of the building's four corners, topped with copper domes. A fire in 1983 destroyed everything but this tower. A small conference room in the base of the tower is used for meetings devoted to veterans' issues.

To the right of the dome is ❻ **Margery Reed Hall,** built in 1929 and named after Mary Reed's daughter. At the time of her death at age 31, she was married to English teacher Paul Mayo, and her name was Margery Reed Mayo. But when the building in her honor was regularly referred to as Mayo Hall, her mother asked that the name be changed to truly recognize her daughter. To the right is the ❼ **Daniels College of Business,** named for Bill Daniels, who was known as "the father of cable television" and donated millions to the school.

Turn left at the second path as it circles the right side of the Carnegie Green. Until 1990 this was the site of the Carnegie Library, the last of the academic libraries funded by Andrew S. Carnegie when it opened in 1908. The campus outgrew that library by the 1930s, and the Mary Reed Library was built. Eventually renovation proved too expensive on the deteriorating building, and it was demolished.

Turn left at the end of the Carnegie Green to walk south and behind the Mary Reed Building. A statue of two women holding a book in the middle of the green is another dedication to Margery Reed by Mary Reed. The waterfall and man-made stream you are walking over is part of the Harper Humanities Garden. The campus is also an arboretum, and this garden is part of the whole landscape, featuring water lilies and reflecting pools.

Evans Chapel and reflecting pool of the Harper Humanities Garden on University of Denver campus

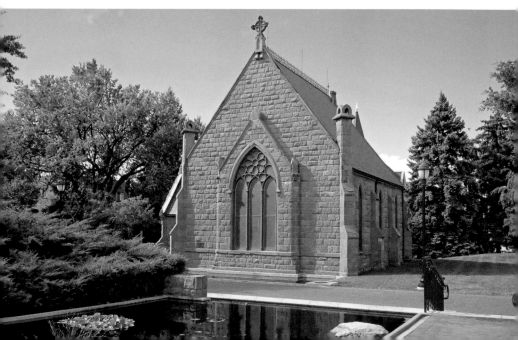

Turn right over the bridge and walk slightly west and then north as the path winds over the water. On your left is the historic ❽ **Evans Chapel.** The University of Denver was founded by John Evans, the second territorial governor of Colorado and founder of Northwestern University in Chicago (Evanston, Illinois, is named for him). "Together with the Methodist Episcopal Church, Evans founded Colorado Seminary, later to become the University of Denver, in 1864," writes Fisher. The Colorado Seminary was first located in downtown Denver and moved to South Denver in the 1880s. The chapel was built as a memorial to Evans's daughter Josephine, who died at age 24. It was moved here brick by brick in 1960 from its original location at 13th Avenue and Bannock Street downtown. The chapel is used for weekly services and is a popular place for weddings on the campus.

Turn right as the path curves toward the Anderson Academic Commons (formerly Penrose Library), the campus's main library, billed as a "true 21st-century library" with computers, fireplaces, a café, and of course, books.

Cross E. Evans Avenue and continue walking north on this block of the campus with the Driscoll University Center (also called the William T. Driscoll Student Center) on your left. If it's a cold day, you can go inside and use the skybridge to cross over E. Evans Avenue instead.

Cross E. Asbury Avenue to the next block of the campus.

Walk to the right of the ❾ **Shwayder Art Building,** named for the Jesse and Nellie Shwayder Foundation. Jesse Shwayder was the founder of the Shwayder Trunk Manufacturing Company in the early 1900s, which became the Samsonite Luggage Company. Inside this 1978 building is the ❿ **Victoria Myhren Gallery** that is open most weekday afternoons and has changing exhibits of local and national artists. Around the side of the building is a fun piece of art, *Whispers,* by former DU professor Lawrence Argent (his *I See What You Mean* blue bear sculpture is seen on Walk 6). Here giant lips on benches invite you to sit down and listen to voices coming up from the grating under your feet.

Directly in front of you, and almost wrapping around you, is the ⓫ **Daniel L. Ritchie Center for Sports and Wellness** with the iconic golden tower (the school colors are crimson and gold). Built in 1999 and named for DU's 16th chancellor, the Ritchie Center tower was modeled after one on the University of Bologna campus in Italy. There are seven athletic venues within and surrounding the Ritchie Center. Inside the tower is the Williams Carillon, 65 chromatically tuned bells that chime every hour.

Turn left just before the front doors of the Ritchie Center and find yourself at the top of the bleacher seats overlooking the soccer and lacrosse fields. Pause to see the view of the Front Range of the Rocky Mountains from this vantage point too.

Walk down the steps toward the field.

Turn left and walk toward E. Asbury Avenue.

Turn right on E. Asbury Avenue. On your right is the **⑫ Merle Catherine Chambers Center for the Advancement of Women,** the current home of the Women's College of Denver, which was founded in 1909 and has had a long relationship with DU.

Turn left on S. High Street and walk to E. Evans Avenue.

Turn right on E. Evans Avenue to leave the campus and get a bite to eat or a drink. One of the oldest campus hangouts is the **⑬ Stadium Inn,** a dive bar with pool tables and other games where students come to blow off a little steam or celebrate team wins. **⑭ Jerusalem Restaurant** has a diner feel with affordable Middle Eastern food that draws people from beyond just the campus. A few doors down is **⑮ Kaladi Coffee Roasters,** with organic and fair-trade coffee and free Wi-Fi.

Turn left on S. Franklin Street and cross E. Evans Avenue.

Note: You can walk 1 mile south on S. Franklin Street to E. Bates Avenue and combine this with Walk 24.

Turn left and walk east on E. Evans Avenue and back toward the campus.

Cross S. University Boulevard as you keep walking east to S. Columbine Street. At the corner of E. Evans Avenue and S. Columbine Street is the historic Buchtel Bungalow, built for the university's third chancellor and now restored to serve as home for the current and future chancellors. According to DU archives, the Craftsman-style bungalow was built between 1905 and 1906 and included a "tuberculosis" porch and sheds for chickens and cows, as well as electric lighting and a coal furnace.

Turn right on S. Columbine Street to walk to E. Warren Avenue.

Turn left on E. Warren Avenue and walk back to Observatory Park where this walk ends.

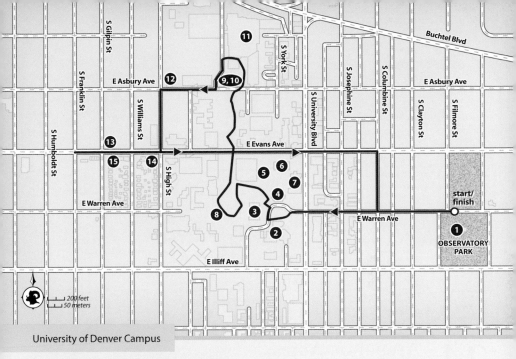

University of Denver Campus

Points of Interest

1. **Chamberlin Observatory** 2930 E. Warren Ave., 303-871-5172, denverastro.org/das/chamberlin-observatory

2. **Iliff School of Theology** 2201 S. University Blvd., iliff.edu

3. **Mary Reed Building** 2199 S. University Blvd.

4. **University Hall**

5. **Buchtel Memorial Tower** 2150 S. Evans Ave.

6. **Margery Reed Hall** 2306 E. Evans Ave.

7. **Daniels College of Business** 2101 S. University Blvd., 303-871-3411, daniels.du.edu

8. **Evans Chapel** University of Denver campus

9. **Shwayder Art Building** 2121 E. Asbury Ave.

10. **Victoria Myhren Gallery** 2121 E. Asbury Ave., 303-871-3716, vicki-myhren-gallery.du.edu

11. **Daniel L. Ritchie Center** 2240 Buchtel Blvd., 303-871-3845, ritchiecenter.du.edu

12. **The Merle Catherine Chambers Center** 1901 E. Asbury Ave., chambersfund.org

13. **Stadium Inn** 1703 E. Evans Ave., 303-733-4031, stadiuminndenver.com

14. **Jerusalem Restaurant** 1890 E. Evans Ave., 303-777-8828, jerusalemrestaurant.com

15. **Kaladi Coffee Roasters** 1730 E. Evans Ave., 720-570-2166, kaladicoffee.com

24 Arapahoe Acres:
A Modern Development

Above: One of the distinctive homes in the Arapahoe Acres subdivision

BOUNDARIES: S. Franklin St., E. Bates Ave., S. Marion St., S. Cornell Cir.
DISTANCE: Approx. 1 mile
DIFFICULTY: Easy
PARKING: Free on-street parking
PUBLIC TRANSIT: The RTD 12 stops at S. Downing St. near Yale Ave. to the west of this walk; the RTD 21 stops near E. Evans Ave. and S. Franklin St. about 1 mile north of this walk.

While there are midcentury modern design houses sprinkled around Denver, and even small enclaves of modernism, Arapahoe Acres is an entire subdivision of midcentury design. One element important to Arapahoe Acres is the Usonian style, once favored by architect Frank Lloyd Wright. Wright's Usonian style was developed during the Depression. In practical terms it meant houses without basements, attics, or ornamentation—a simpler version of his Prairie style. There is also an emphasis on natural materials such as stone and wood and an earth tone palette. Arapahoe Acres was the vision of developer and builder Edward Hawkins, who began the project on the edge of the suburb of Englewood in 1949. Hawkins hired architect Eugene Sternberg, who taught architecture and planning at the University of Denver and had an interest in stylish, affordable housing. In eight years Arapahoe Acres was dreamed, built, and embraced by people who also had an appreciation for the simple designs that featured private exteriors and open, flowing interior floor plans, all for an affordable price. This tour takes you through the inner winding streets of this unique subdivision.

All of the homes in Arapahoe Acres are privately owned, so it is not possible to go inside them on this tour. However, sometimes there are fundraising walking tours (for example, proceeds from a tour might go to a neighborhood school) when a few homeowners welcome curious strangers into their homes. Also, open houses when a place is for sale provide an opportunity to see the interiors and backyards of these unique homes.

Walk Description

Begin this walk on the corner of S. Marion Street and E. Bates Avenue. Wooden signs mark the boundaries of Arapahoe Acres, and each one has an orange triangle for the letter A like an arrowhead. This tiny detail recognizes the Arapahoe tribe from which the name comes. ❶ **The house on the corner at 2900 S. Marion Street** was the model home for Arapahoe Acres. Diane Wray, Arapahoe Acres resident and cofounder of the Modern Architecture Preservation League, wrote a book, *Arapahoe Acres: An Architectural History, 1949–1957*, detailing the architectural history of this neighborhood. Her in-depth research and sometimes clinical detail are the basis for this walking tour.

By the time the first model home was ready to show, the first nine houses built in Arapahoe Acres were already sold. Still, about 4,000 people came to the open house in March 1950, Wray writes in her book. Arapahoe Acres is the first post–World War II residential subdivision listed as a historic district in the National Register of Historic Places, states the site, arapahoeacres.org.

According to Wray, of the 124 homes that make up Arapahoe Acres, only 20 homes were built exactly to Sternberg's plans. Wray describes Sternberg's initial willingness to partner with Hawkins, "because of his interest in the creation of socially-conscious modern housing combining quality architectural design and economical construction." Sternberg split with Hawkins over the sale of this model home, Wray writes, for $11,500 over the original agreed-upon price. The

Sternberg homes are primarily along S. Marion Street. "Stylistically, Sternberg's work was related to the International Style," explains Wray. What is also retained from Sternberg's work is the overall layout of Arapahoe Acres. "Houses were oriented on their lots for privacy, and to take the best advantage of southern and western exposures for solar heating and mountain views," explains Wray. "Sternberg's plan reduced traffic, resulting in a safer, quieter neighborhood."

Hawkins and his wife, Charlotte Hawkins, lived in the house at 2910 S. Marion Street and others you will see on the tour. From the corner, proceed south on Marion Street.

Turn left on E. Cornell Avenue. Note that the next three streets share the same name. Wray explains the reason for the street names: Bates College in Lewiston, Maine; Cornell University in Ithaca, New York; and Dartmouth University in Hanover, New Hampshire. This reflects the neighborhood's connection to the University of Denver and its connection to the east.

After Sternberg left, Hawkins took over the design. "Hawkins homes were built within the original Sternberg site plan," writes Wray. "But to Hawkins, style took precedence over economy." What this means is you will notice larger and more elaborately designed homes on the rest of the tour.

Turn right on S. Cornell Circle. In 1951, Hawkins hired architect Jerry Dion to work part time and complete Arapahoe Acres. Dion had graduated from the University of Denver's School of Architecture and Planning and was also a fan of Wright's work. Dion worked on 35 of the homes, and his own was at ❷ 3059 S. Cornell Circle. Wray writes that Dion took the job with Hawkins "in order to earn a down payment for his own home in Arapahoe Acres."

Clever signs mark this historical neighborhood.

Turn left as the street ends in a cul-de-sac on the right.

Turn left again as the street ends and curves.

Turn left on E. Cornell Place and walk west. Sternberg's plans for a private neighborhood park on this street within Arapahoe Acres were later scrapped by Hawkins. The house at ❸ 1411 E. Cornell Place was designed by local architect Peter Looms for use as his own residence.

Turn right on E. Cornell Avenue and walk north to S. Lafayette Drive.

Turn left and cross E. Cornell Avenue to walk north on S. Lafayette Drive. The two-story house at ❹ **2980 S. Lafayette Drive** with the red door was the last house constructed in Arapahoe Acres in 1957 and the residence of Edward Hawkins and his wife for 10 years. There are many Japanese touches on this house—the roof, the railing, even the red door and pruned evergreen shrubs. It may still have a backyard in-ground pool that was part of Hawkins's design. Because he had eliminated all plans for a neighborhood park, Wray states that Hawkins would open his backyard pool to children in the neighborhood on summer Saturdays.

This block is about the highest point on this walk, and the second-story homes get a view of the tips of the Rocky Mountain peaks to the west. You can also get a glimpse of them as you walk here.

In her research Wray learned that a group of Arapahoe Acres homeowners hired Stanley J. Yoshimura to design the Japanese gardens to complement the houses in the 1960s. Yoshimura designed the yard at ❺ **2960 S. Lafayette Drive.** Wray also points out a group of three houses "united by a stack bond concrete block wall" for addresses 2923, 2919, and 2915 S. Lafayette Drive.

Turn left as the street bends and walk west.

Turn right and walk north to E. Bates Avenue.

Turn left on E. Bates Avenue and walk back to S. Marion Street.

Note: By turning right on E. Bates Avenue and walking east to S. Franklin Street, then 1 mile north on S. Franklin Street to E. Evans Avenue, you can combine this walk with Walk 23.

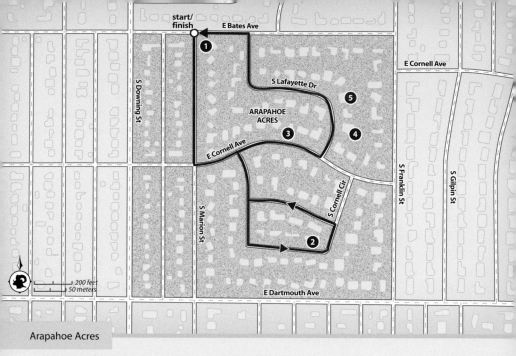

Point of Interest

Arapahoe Acres arapahoeacreshistoricdistrict.org

1 2900 S. Marion St.

2 3059 S. Cornell Circle

3 1411 E. Cornell Place

4 2980 S. Lafayette Drive

5 2960 S. Lafayette Drive

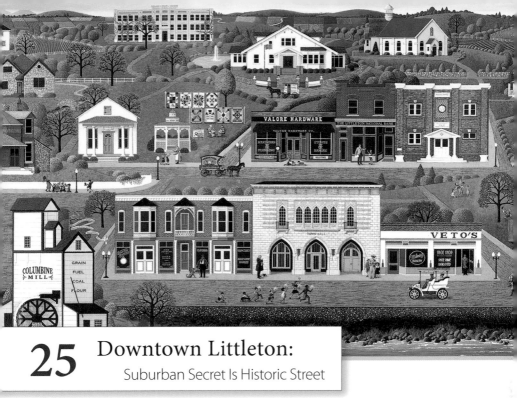

25 Downtown Littleton:
Suburban Secret Is Historic Street

Above: Passages *mural by local artist Michelle Lamb adorns the old train depot.*
photographed by Michelle Lamb

BOUNDARIES: Main St., S. Rio Grande St., W. Alamo Ave.
DISTANCE: 0.75 mile
DIFFICULTY: Easy
PARKING: Free parking is available along Main St.
PUBLIC TRANSIT: RTD light-rail orange and green lines stop in Downtown Littleton.

The scene: a clear blue sky overhead, warmth from the bright October afternoon sun, and a clear view of the Rocky Mountains with a fresh dusting of snow on the peaks. A group of women and their daughters are laughing together as they cross the street and wait for a table for lunch, while around the corner two friends step into a local bookstore, and the patio at the restaurant next door is completely full for lunch. A couple of blocks away grandparents take their grandchildren out for pizza, a young couple holds hands while walking along, and two women come out of a yoga class chatting. This sums up a day in downtown Littleton, a suburb of Denver that has this quaint historic street tucked off from a busy highway and the acres of suburban homes all around.

Walk Description

Begin the walk at the RTD light-rail stop on W. Alamo Avenue. It is less than a 20-minute drive from downtown Denver to downtown Littleton, with mostly highway driving, but it's ideal to take the light-rail and not worry about traffic or parking. Plus, departing from the train gives you a chance to check out the historic Littleton train depot (aka Denver & Rio Grande Railroad Depot), now a coffee shop. This stone building was erected in 1875 to replace a wood-frame depot.

In Stephen J. Leonard and Thomas J. Noel's book *Denver: Mining Camp to Metropolis,* they describe how Littleton came to be. Richard Little came to Denver in 1860, bought land in this agricultural area, and also homesteaded. By 1867, he had started the Rough and Ready Flour Mill and by 1872 platted the town that was modeled on the New Hampshire village he grew up in. Little had been working on the City Ditch (see Walk 20) and then decided he liked the country-side enough to put down roots.

Cross Alamo Avenue walking north.

Join S. Rio Grande Street and walk north to Main Street. (Suggested detour here if you don't mind a busier street and intersection. Follow Alamo Avenue east [uphill] as it turns into W. Littleton Boulevard. Turn left on S. Court Place and walk past the historic Arapahoe County Courthouse to the Depot Art Gallery, which includes a caboose as an art gallery.)

You will walk past or through tiny Bega Park, named after Bega, Australia, which has a sister city relationship with Littleton.

Turn left on Main Street to walk west. You will already see the purplish-blue of the Rocky Mountains to the west as you begin this walk of historic buildings that now house shops, restaurants, and other businesses.

As you cross Sycamore Street look right to see that neighborhood staple: the Irish pub. ❶ **Ned Kelly's** is the answer here in Littleton—for beer mostly, but there is a limited food menu.

Shops to the left of me, shops to the right of me. I love mixing an outdoor stroll with retail therapy. With a hot pink exterior it's a given that the women's clothing and accessories in ❷ **Details Boutique,** on your right, are colorful. That pink nearly screams Betsey Johnson, but really there are tamer labels like 3 Dot, Big Star, Free People, LeLe, and hip Old Gringo cowgirl boots.

If it's lunchtime, consider the affordable ❸ **Pho Real,** on your right, for casual Vietnamese cuisine.

At Prince Street, look right for **4** **Spur Coffee** and **5** **Inside Scoop Creamery** (love that clever name!) for a pick-me-up of the caffeine and/or sugar sort.

On the left at this intersection is **6** **Willow: An Artisan's Market** (to the left), which reminds me of the Artisan Center in Cherry Creek North (see Walk 19) with a mix of whimsical gift items for babies, gardens, Christmas trees, and the like. Next door is the **7** **Olde Towne Tavern,** an updated version of the American diner with microbrews and burgers.

Across the street is Curds Cheese, the place for your charcuterie trays, sandwiches, and a respectable selection of cheeses.

Plan to loop back to **8** **The Alley** for a late lunch or even dinner if you're in the mood for Mexican at this combination food truck and bar.

It's not like tea is some trendy new drink, but I do like to see the many ways people repackage the tea experience. At **9** **In-Tea,** they have experts (tea-ologists?) who help you find your perfect blend, which can be enjoyed with a sandwich or a pastry.

At the corner with Nevada Street, the **10** **Town Hall Arts Center** is a beautifully restored 1920 former municipal building designed by architect J. J. B. Benedict, who also designed and

donated the light fixtures you see on the front of the building. According to the City of Littleton historical records, the design is a combination of Italian Renaissance and Gothic Revival, with Colorado symbols such as the state flower, columbine, and eagles in the window details. Since the 1980s it has been home to local theatre productions and concerts.

Downtown Littleton's historic Town Hall building

While it seems normal to go into a cheese shop like Curds, it is not every day that I wander into a meat shop. **11** **La Vaca Meat Company** has a cute little storefront here, offering steaks and other cuts from ranches in Colorado and Texas.

As you cross Nevada Street, look right and make note of **12** **Kate's Wine Bar** for a stop later in the day or evening.

13 **Austin/Hauck** is that rare boutique devoted solely to men's clothing, both business and casual, as well as shoes and accessories.

Backstory: Who's That Architect?

Jules Jacques Benoit (J. J. B.) Benedict was one of Denver's foremost architects in the early 1900s. But he was also well known in Littleton, where he lived with his wife not far from Main Street. The house Benedict designed for himself was actually a country estate that they called Wyldemere Farms; it has been used as a Carmelite Monastery since 1947. The chapel—the Benedicts' former living room—is open for Sunday Mass, but otherwise the property is not open to the public.

Benedict's best-known work in Denver includes the Washington Park Boating Pavilion (see Walk 20), Woodbury Branch Library (see Walk 9), the Denver Botanic Gardens administrative offices designed as a private home (see Walk 18), and the residence at 360 High Street designed for Thomas Sewell, a mining engineer and son of a former Colorado governor (see Walk 19).

Learn more about Benedict and the history of this suburb at the Littleton Museum (6028 S. Gallup St., 303-795-3950, littletongov.org/museum), which is about 1.5 miles from Main Street and near Benedict's former home.

Finally, chocolate is recognized as therapy! **⓮ The Chocolate Therapist** is where they embrace the idea that chocolate is good for you, so you should indulge and enjoy. I'll be back.

You could easily miss **⓯ Café Terracotta,** a half block down on S. Curtice Street in a restored Victorian house, but don't. This place easily fills up for breakfast, lunch, and dinner, even with the patio open on nice days.

Main Street comes to an end at Littleton's historic library, which was originally designed by architect J. J. B. Benedict as the town library in the Beaux Arts architectural style. This library was also used as a fire station, dance hall, jail, and movie theater, and has been a restaurant for several years. Looking south you will see the historic flour mill building that is now a restaurant too.

Turn around to walk east on Main Street and back to the light-rail station.

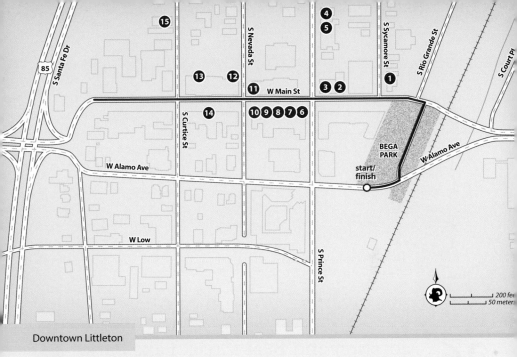

Downtown Littleton

Points of Interest

1. **Ned Kelly's Irish Pub** 5686 S. Sycamore St., Littleton, 720-283-8717, nedkellysirishpub.com

2. **Details Boutique** 2359 W. Main St., Littleton, 303-703-3884, detailsboutique.com

3. **Pho Real** 2399 W. Main St., 720-638-6884

4. **Spur Coffee** 5624 S. Prince St., 303-997-2209, spurcoffee.com

5. **Inside Scoop Creamery** 5654 S. Prince St., 303-798-4768, insidescoopdenver.com

6. **Willow** 2400 W. Main St., Littleton, 303-730-8521, willowartisansmarket.com

7. **Olde Towne Tavern** 2410 W. Main St., 303-794-4329, ottlittleton.com

8. **The Alley** 2420 W. Main St. #110, 720-316-8002, littletonalley.com

9. **In-Tea** 2440 W. Main St., 720-981-2512, in-tea.net

10. **Town Hall Arts Center** 2450 Main St., Littleton, 303-794-2787, townhallartscenter.org

11. **La Vaca Meat Company** 2489 W. Main St., 720-502-4400, lavacameat.com

12. **Kate's Wine Bar** 5671 S. Nevada St., 303-999-2895, kateswinebar.wixsite.com/kate-site

13. **Austin/Hauck** 2569 W. Main St., Littleton, 303-730-7778, austinhauck.com

14. **The Chocolate Therapist** 2560 W. Main St., 303-795-7913, thechocolatetherapist.com

15. **Café Terracotta** 5649 S. Curtice St., Littleton, 303-794-6054, cafe-terracotta.com

26 Morrison and Bear Creek Lake Park:
A River Runs Through It

Above: *Enjoy the soothing sound of Bear Creek during a stroll through Morrison.*

BOUNDARIES: Bear Creek Ave., Park Ave., Bear Creek Lake Park
DISTANCE: Approx. 3 miles
DIFFICULTY: Moderate
PARKING: Free 3-hour parking is available along Bear Creek Ave. in Morrison.
PUBLIC TRANSIT: RTD 2X bus stops at Morrison Park Loop.

The small town of Morrison is a short drive from downtown Denver and the gateway town to Red Rocks Park and Amphitheatre. Morrison has a charm all its own and plenty to offer for a nature lover's little day trip. With a population of fewer than 500 people, Morrison is genuinely tiny and feels like a world away from the skyscrapers of the Mile High City. From the old-fashioned downtown, you can easily walk alongside Bear Creek over to Bear Creek Lake Park, where you can check out a few trails. Loop back and you will have plenty of good restaurants to choose from for lunch or dinner, some with views of the foothills or next to the creek.

Walk Description

Begin this walk at ❶ **Memory Plaza** next to the Park Avenue bridge where Bear Creek Avenue and Park Avenue meet.

Walk east on the path alongside Bear Creek. With Morrison's little downtown on your left and the creek on your right, the water is at its most musical as it rushes over the rocks and downstream.

Look up as you cross the bridge to see the old Morrison School bell. A sign on your left tells the history of the school, the bell, and how it ended up hanging on this bridge.

Just after the bridge on your left is a possible detour to take now or on the return. You will see a mural with Morrison's highlights—geology (red rocks) and paleontology (dinosaurs), famous musicians (Red Rocks again), railroads, outdoor recreation, mining, and the town founders. The kiosk next to the mural has historic photos and details about the importance of the railroad and supplies for miners as the town developed.

Across the street is the ❷ **Mill Street Eats,** where you can stop in for a hearty sandwich, beer, or ice cream after your walk. On this side of the street is ❸ **The Cow: An Eatery** (formerly Blue Cow Eatery), with a very desirable patio area next to Bear Creek. This casual diner is open for breakfast and "linner" with burgers and a kids' menu.

Quite a few of Morrison's restaurants are just across Bear Creek Avenue and have been there for decades—part of the scenery like Red Rocks Park and Amphitheatre. ❹ **Tony Rigatoni's Italian Kitchen** has cornered the market on pizza and pasta in town and also has a little patio to enjoy on warm days. And then there is ❺ **Cafe Prague** for those hungry for schnitzel and goulash. Really, the restaurant's reputation is such that it draws diners from Denver who want a fabulous meal on a date night. This place is more than just a stopover on the way to or from Red Rocks Park and Amphitheatre. Upscale contemporary Latin food is on the menu at ❻ **Beso de Arte** in a little historic building with a pretty garden patio. It is another unexpected culinary experience in Morrison that goes well beyond Tex-Mex. ❼ **The Morrison Inn** also has an enviable location with its patio's view to the west that is perfect for watching the sunset over a couple of margaritas and some Mexican food.

Turn right when the path forks about one-half block after Soda Lakes Road.

Turn left and continue walking east on the path that is on the north side of Bear Creek. You will walk under CO 470, and Bear Creek Lake Park is on the other side. Note that there is a fee to drive into the park, but it's free to walk or bicycle in on the trails.

Turn right when you see the bridge over Bear Creek. It's a nice spot to stop and look west up the creek.

Turn left shortly after crossing the bridge and leave the concrete path for a dirt trail on the creek's south side.

Walk east on the dirt path. In early fall this path will likely be carpeted with golden cottonwood leaves that will crackle underfoot. And in summer those trees can provide wonderful shade for this walk.

Kid Tip: Not only do you hear and see the creek as you're walking along this trail, but when you cross the bridge your whole family can also walk down to the creek, and maybe feel the cold water with fingers and toes. Best on hot summer days!

You can also ride a bike in Bear Creek Lake Park.

Veer right toward the Skunk Hollow area with picnic tables, parking, and a bathroom, and cross the pavement to the road. There is a trail map here if you are curious to get a park overview before joining the trails.

Cross the road walking east and go a short distance to a trailhead with markers.

Turn right to take the Owl Trail. This trail leads to the ❽ **Bear Creek Lake Park Visitor Center,** where you can go inside and learn about the animals and plants that thrive on this land. There are also maps to guide you around the entire 2,600-acre park where there are three lakes—one just for swimming, others for boating; miles of trails for horseback riders, cyclists, and pedestrians/runners; and several campsites. The lakes provide that little bit of beach Denverites are sometimes craving in the summer months, with sand, a playground, and a snack bar. Birders can also get a list of the many migratory birds they can view and hear in the park, particularly near Bear Creek Reservoir, where there are herons, warblers, hummingbirds, pheasants, and many more.

Backstory: A Dining Destination

The Fort Restaurant (19192 CO 8, 303-697-4771, thefort.com) is a destination in itself in Morrison. No matter how famous the clientele—from movie actors to world leaders—the real star at this restaurant is the award-winning food that celebrates the West. Bison is prepared in totally unique ways, such as sausage, marrowbones, filet mignon, stew, tongue, and ribs. Or move on to the other game and fowl on the menu, all with a little jalapeño here or chipotle there. It's a mix of Native American, Southwestern, and contemporary flavors that is beyond compare.

The place gets its name from the unique building the owners constructed—a historic adobe fort. This place is one great story after another—they used to have a bear who lived here, they tomahawk open the champagne, and this was the owners' house. There is a gift shop near the entrance, and there are annual events here, including a Native American powwow.

Turn left with the trail as it now goes north. This exposed prairie can be a good spot to soak in a little sunshine on a winter's day walk.

Turn right and walk briefly on the Mount Carbon Trail.

Turn left to walk on the Owl Trail again as it heads downhill toward Bear Creek.

Turn left again as the trail becomes parallel to Bear Creek and you loop back toward Morrison. Cross the road and Skunk Hollow again to rejoin the dirt path going west.

Turn right just before Soda Lake Road to get on the path as it becomes parallel to CO 8/Morrison Road (which is then Bear Creek Avenue in Morrison).

Turn left and continue walking west into Morrison and end the walk back at Memory Plaza—with a stop for ice cream at Mill Street Eats, of course!

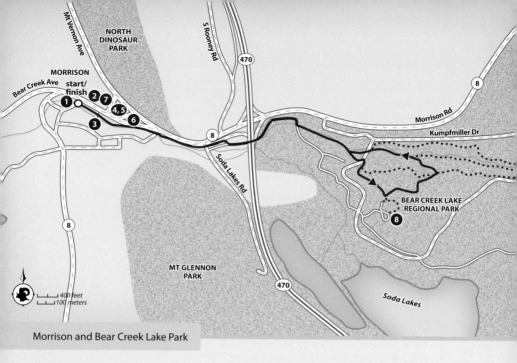

Morrison and Bear Creek Lake Park

Points of Interest

1. **Memory Plaza** Bear Creek and Park Avenues
2. **Mill Street Eats** 401 Bear Creek Ave., Morrison, 303-697-1700
3. **The Cow: An Eatery** 316 Bear Creek Ave., Morrison, 303-697-5721, thecoweatery.com
4. **Tony Rigatoni's** 215 Bear Creek Ave., Morrison, 303-697-5508, tonyrigatonis.com
5. **Cafe Prague** 209 Bear Creek Ave., Morrison, 303-697-9722, thecafeprague.com
6. **Beso de Arte** 102 Market St., Morrison, 303-697-3377, besodearte.com
7. **Morrison Inn** 301 Bear Creek Ave., Morrison, 303-697-6650
8. **Bear Creek Lake Park Visitor Center** 15600 W. Morrison Rd., 303-697-6159, lakewood.org

27 Red Rocks Park and Amphitheatre:
One Concert Venue, Add Nature Trails

Above: Fitness buffs use the seats at Red Rocks Amphitheatre for working out on non-concert days.

BOUNDARIES: W. Alameda Pkwy., Ship Rock Rd., Trading Post Rd.
DISTANCE: Approx. 2.5 miles
DIFFICULTY: Moderate to difficult
PARKING: Free parking is available in all parking lots.
PUBLIC TRANSIT: None

Red Rocks Park and Amphitheatre is famous worldwide. Well, maybe just the amphitheatre is famous. And for good reason—U2, the Grateful Dead, the Beatles, Sting, Jimi Hendrix, and just about every great rock musician has not only performed here but also raved about doing so. It is a one-of-a-kind acoustically perfect natural amphitheatre in a spectacular setting. Of the 868 acres that make up Red Rocks Park, the amphitheatre is just one part. There are hiking, biking, and horseback riding trails, which also afford views of the slanted and towering red rocks.

Trading Post Trail is a 1.4-mile loop that is easy enough for children to do. This walk combines the Trading Post Trail with a walk through the amphitheatre, which has a lot of stairs, and at an altitude of 6,450 feet above sea level it can be quite strenuous.

Note: Red Rocks Park and Amphitheatre is closed on concert dates while the stage is set up. Always check their calendar or call first to make sure you have access. Also, use caution when crossing roads, as cars share the roads with pedestrians and cyclists within Red Rocks Park. Check the weather, as you don't want to be here during a thunderstorm.

Walk Description

Start this walk in the Upper North Lot—you'll be doing a lot of stair climbing and trail walking, so you don't need to park any farther away than necessary. There is little to no shade on this walk, so bring water, sunscreen, and a hat.

Walk south on the path leading to the amphitheatre. The terrace at the top of the amphitheatre is the roof of the visitor center and ❶ **Ship Rock Grille,** but these places are not subterranean, and like everyplace at Red Rocks there is gorgeous scenery to see. Inside the ❷ **Red Rocks Visitor Center** is the ❸ **Colorado Music Hall of Fame,** showing off the many big-name musicians who have played at Red Rocks Amphitheatre over the decades. It's a very impressive lineup that makes you want to see a show here. Or you can just see a sample of all that history by watching a documentary about Red Rocks with concert footage in the Southwest Heart of the Rock Theatre. In addition, there are exhibits about the unique geology of Red Rocks and the surrounding area, where many dinosaur bones and other fossils have been discovered.

As you are crossing the terrace to the south side of the ❹ **amphitheatre,** stop and take in the natural beauty that inspired this concert venue. It's a terrific view of Denver to the east right over Dinosaur Ridge (see Walk 28). The bench seats are framed by Creation Rock to the left (as you are facing the stage) and Ship Rock to the right. Each of these red sandstone rocks is taller than Niagara Falls. Signs all over Red Rocks remind people not to climb on the rocks; they can be very slippery.

Remember John Brisben Walker from Walk 7 and his former castle by the South Platte River? Walker was a dreamer, and one of his visions was to make Red Rocks a world-class outdoor music hall. Back then he called it "Garden of the Titans." Walker owned this land and between 1906 and 1910 produced concerts in this natural acoustic setting on a temporary stage. In the 1920s, another visionary convinced Denver city leaders to buy Walker's land and turn it into a real concert venue. Red Rocks Park and Amphitheatre is owned and operated by the city of Denver to this day.

Come see a show at Red Rocks Park and Amphitheatre.
photographed by Steve Crecelius/Visit Denver

Architect Burnham Hoyt (whose residential work was highlighted in Walk 18) was hired in the 1930s to design the amphitheatre, and in 1947 it was opened for an Easter Sunrise Service (the Easter service still takes place, depending on the fickle Colorado spring weather). The beauty of Hoyt's design is how natural it looks. In fact, the rows of benches were once a boulder field that had to be dynamited and moved piece by piece. Manpower from the federally sponsored Civilian Conservation Corps and the Work Projects Administration were brought on to make the project affordable. From planning to completion, it took 12 years to finish building the Red Rocks Amphitheatre. The roof over the stage was added later and is not part of the original design.

Kid Tip: If you're interested in music and/or beautifully natural geological formations, then Red Rocks is a jackpot for you. With an extensive history of amazing bands and artists, the outdoor concert hall is framed by large (slanting) red rocks that gave Red Rocks its name, and fame. I love the Beatles, and they played here—see if your favorite band has too.

Descend the stairs. Chances are you will have a lot of company on the stairs because Red Rocks is also a very popular (unofficial) outdoor gym. At 6,400 feet above sea level, this is one intense StairMaster workout!

Turn right for the south ramp/South Parking Lot, which is a long elevated ramp and stairs down to Ship Rock Road.

Cross Ship Rock Road and walk a few feet south from the stairs you just descended and up to Nine Parks Rock and the Trading Post.

Turn right and follow the trail as it curves and winds through more glorious jutting red rocks. Kind of like looking at clouds drifting by, you can stop and ponder the names assigned to each rock formation. On your right, in this order, will be Iceberg Rock, Sinking Titanic Rock, Sphinx Rock, Gog Rock, Magog Rock, and, after the trail turns right, on your left will be Frog Rock.

When you come to a slight hilltop overlooking Picnic Rock and several trails leading downhill to it, resist temptation and turn right at the concrete barricade. It is safe and pretty to look at down there, but it is not the Trading Post Trail.

As the trail continues south through an open meadow you will notice cactus and yucca plants mixed in with the grasses—a reminder of being on the arid plains. You'll certainly hear birds on this walk and maybe even see some deer or snakes.

Go left as the trail turns and begins to loop back. If it's a weekday during the school year, you might hear children playing at recess at the elementary school nearby.

By now you have probably seen a few signs marking a closed trail. This can be confusing—and you will see a lot more of these up ahead, accompanied by repeated requests to not climb on the rocks—but rest assured that Trading Post Trail itself is not closed. Those well-worn paths that are now closed are not part of this trail.

After you pass Park Cave Rock and Frog Rock on your left (by the way, the names for these rock formations are not actually on or near the rocks but only on maps), cross the road and continue walking north.

Just around Picnic Rock on your left is the **⑤ Trading Post,** where you can get snacks, water, T-shirts, shot glasses, CDs, and other Red Rocks souvenirs. There is also a Colorado Welcome Center inside with walls of brochures and trail maps for all over the state. The Trading Post actually predates the amphitheatre and was built here in 1931. The back porch has incredible views and places to sit and rest. During one walk here we stumbled on a Broncos-themed wedding on the green out back (as in the Denver Broncos football team).

Walk north on Trading Post Road past Stage Rock and up the ramp and stairs on the north side of the amphitheatre.

Climb the amphitheatre steps back up to the terrace.

Veer right to take the path back to the Upper North Lot and complete this walk—maybe with lunch at the Ship Rock Grille.

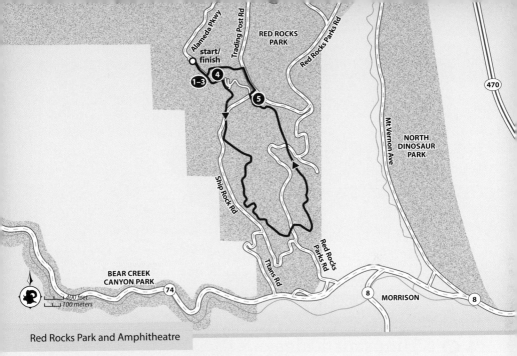

Red Rocks Park and Amphitheatre

Points of Interest

1 Ship Rock Grille 18300 W. Alameda Pkwy., 303-697-4939 ext. 111, redrocksonline.com

2 Red Rocks Visitor Center 18300 W. Alameda Pkwy., 303-697-4939, redrocksonline.com

3 Colorado Music Hall of Fame 18300 W. Alameda Pkwy., 303-697-4939, redrocksonline.com

4 Red Rocks Amphitheatre 18300 W. Alameda Pkwy., 720-865-2494, redrocksonline.com

5 Red Rocks Trading Post 17900 Trading Post Rd., 303-697-6910, redrocksonline.com

28 Dinosaur Ridge:
Road to the First Settlers

Above: Dinosaurs once roamed the land that is now a steep hillside overlooking Denver.

BOUNDARIES: W. Alameda Pkwy.
DISTANCE: 2.25 miles
DIFFICULTY: Moderate
PARKING: Free parking is available at the visitor center or in the gravel parking lot.
PUBLIC TRANSIT: None

Long, long before Native Americans, gold miners, or any people at all lived in Colorado, this area was a mangrove swamp populated by dinosaurs. And while you have heard of the Gold Rush, you may not have heard of the Great Dinosaur Rush that happened several years later. In both instances, the rush was more of a plunder with natural resources rapidly extracted from these mountains and foothills. What you will see on this walk are footprints, bulges, ripples, and other evidence of that time 150 million years ago that could not be chipped out and hauled away. The signs along the road provide illustrations of what these massive creatures must have looked like when in their native swamp habitat, giving your imagination a few images to work with as you look at the rocks. Brontosaurus (also known as Apatosaurus), stegosaurus (now the Colorado state fossil), diplodocus, and allosaurus were all discovered here in 1877.

Note: Bring water, sunscreen, and a hat for this totally exposed walk up a steep hill.

Walk Description

Start at the base of the road where the gates keep vehicles (except for guided tour buses) out. There are lanes designated on the road for bicyclers, for pedestrians, and the shuttle buses. You can park at the ❶ **Dinosaur Ridge Visitor Center** and walk up the road to the gate, but it does add a half-mile round-trip to the walk.

Stop in at the visitor center (souvenirs, books, and brochure guides for sale) and the exhibit hall (scientific displays) as part of your visit here. (If you are combining this with the walk at Red Rocks Park and Amphitheatre, you can enter from the opposite side, but then you might miss the visitor center.)

The Dinosaur Ridge Exhibit Hall on the east side of the visitor center shows off fossils from the area and has replicas of animals that would have lived here—these are all hands-on displays meant to be touched and explored by children and their grown-ups. Keep in mind that the visitor center parking lot closes and gates are locked at the end of the day.

All of the information for this walk was provided courtesy of the Friends of Dinosaur Ridge, the nonprofit group that preserves this area for educational purposes.

Kid Tip: Even if you don't see an entire dinosaur, then you will without a doubt see bone fragments, such as legs. At the crest of the hill, there is something in the rock that appears to be an unhatched egg. Is it really an egg, or just a perfect rocky formation? No one knows! It's a geologic mystery. Also, even though you aren't exactly walking in their footsteps, you can put your hands in some of the dinosaur footprints here.

A small gravel parking lot lies on the east side of W. Alameda Parkway, just before the private road to Rooney Ranch, where you can park during your walk also. The Rooney family homesteaded the ranch in the 1860s, and it is on the National Register of Historic Places. Rooney family members still live on this working ranch. The Dinosaur Ridge Visitor Center was built as a house on the ranch in the 1950s.

Walk on the right shoulder of the road as you begin your ascent. Yes, ascent. It is uphill all the way to the top on this walk.

Dinosaur Ridge was first discovered by fossil hunters in the late 1800s, and they dug out many impressive dinosaur bones that were sent off to museums. In the 1930s the Alameda Parkway was built and made the fossils more evident and accessible.

Given how exposed this hillside is, the best time to visit Dinosaur Ridge is morning or late afternoon. It can be very hot up here in the summer on this walk—a stark contrast to the swampy remains of leafy trees and tidal waters you'll be walking alongside.

This hill is called a hogback, which has lifted up so that one side of the ridge is younger than the other and each represents a different geologic time period. When dinosaurs roamed the earth, the slanting rocks were flat underneath their giant feet. To your right on this hogback you will see piles of chipped shale. One cool thing about walking this trail instead of being driven up it is that you can pause in this stretch and stare at the shale in hopes of spotting a fossil or some kind of plant or animal marine life (any fossil or rock collecting is prohibited). During the Cretaceous time, about 100 million years ago, this was a shoreline, and the Benton shales are evidence of submarine deposit.

After the shale deposits end, there are some bumpy rocks. These "ripples" in the rock are part of the ❷ **mangrove swamp** that was here so long ago. It's like seeing a forever frozen itty-bitty wave. You will see the impression left by a tree limb in one rock.

It's fitting that you are hearing the low hum of the freeway from down below because, based on the abundance of dinosaur footprints for hundreds of miles in either direction along what is known as the Dakota Group, this area is nicknamed the Dinosaur Freeway. Scientists speculate it may have been part of a migration route.

The highlights of this walk are the ❸ **dinosaur tracks.** There are benches and an elevated viewing station installed here—the only place on the walk to stop and rest on the east side of the trail. The footprints have been enhanced with black to make them easier to see. The three-toed prints were made by an Iguanodon-like dinosaur—there is a replica of one outside the visitor center—that walked on all fours. There are more than 300 tracks left here by several different dinosaurs.

As you go around the bend in the road, you travel back in time another 50 million years to the Late Jurassic era. Just after the turn is a

See where dinosaurs roamed!

Backstory: Looking for More Fossils?

Not quite walking distance, but a short drive away from Dinosaur Ridge, is the Morrison Natural History Museum (501 CO 8, 303-697-1873, mnhm.org), with even more fossils and guided tours available. Some of the bones from Arthur Lakes's digs are on display at this museum, and others are still being extracted from the hard rock on site. Dinosaur Ridge is certainly an important geologic site, but at this museum you learn how it is just one piece of a much larger area of dinosaur history.

mysterious round rock within the straight layers of rock. Although some people call it a dinosaur egg, it is too big for that explanation. Another ❹ **Mesozoic mystery!**

Walk downhill toward the end of the road. Again, steps and raised areas have been installed to make it easier to see the subtle dinosaur impressions left behind. Rather than coastline, this rock shows a time of river channels and floodplains. It's described as being like "the side of a closed book" rather than the "open book" of the visible footprints.

❺ **The Brontosaur Bulge** is an example of this closed book. Here the incredible weight of the Brontosaurus left foot-deep indentations in the sediment, and they are almost hanging in the rock today.

The ❻ **Dinosaur Bone Quarry site** is the end of the trail. This is where Arthur Lakes, a teacher at the Colorado School of Mines in Golden (see Walk 29), began digging for fossils in 1877. His digging led to the bone wars or Great Dinosaur Rush, when suddenly everyone wanted to find dinosaur bones for museums. At the time Lakes was working for a Yale professor and found the remains of stegosaurus, apatosaurus, and diplodocus dinosaurs. These bones may have been washed down an ancient riverbed and later fossilized into the rocks. This is just one of more than a dozen quarry sites in the Morrison Formation (a huge sequence of sedimentary rock rich with dinosaur fossils).

Turn around and retrace your steps to walk back down the road—maybe pausing at a viewing station to the east—to the gate to end this walk.

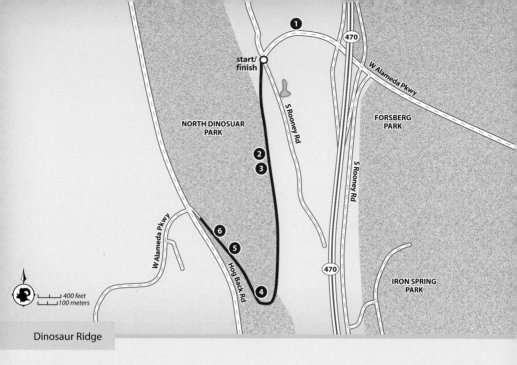

Dinosaur Ridge

Point of Interest

1. **Dinosaur Ridge Visitor Center and Exhibit Hall** 16831 W. Alameda Pkwy., 303-697-3466, dinoridge.org
2. Mangrove swamp
3. Dinosaur tracks
4. Mesozoic mystery
5. The Brontosaur Bulge
6. Dinosaur Bone Quarry site

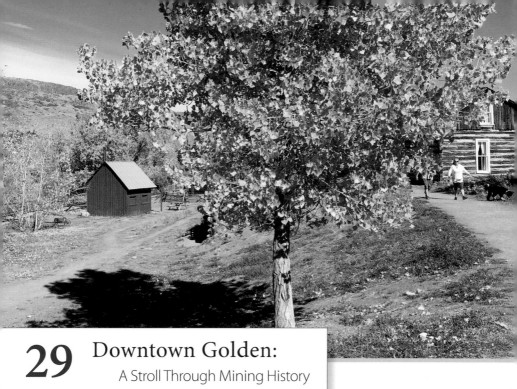

29 Downtown Golden:
A Stroll Through Mining History

Above: *Golden's Clear Creek History Park*

BOUNDARIES: 15th St., Illinois St., 10th St., Washington Ave.
DISTANCE: 1 mile
DIFFICULTY: Easy
PARKING: Free parking is available on side streets; fee parking lots are on campus and on 15th St. (note permit-only parking areas on campus streets).
PUBLIC TRANSIT: The RTD GS Regional bus makes stops in downtown Golden. The W light-rail line goes from Union Station to Golden (note you will be south of downtown where this walk takes place and will need to walk to the start of the route, about 2.5 miles).

A 1-mile walk in downtown Golden is a very condensed version of several walks in Denver: creekside paths, historical museums and other buildings, art galleries, shops, restaurants, and parks. Officially founded in 1859 by gold-seeking miners, Golden's history is very similar to that of Denver, and for five years Golden City was the capital of the Territory of Colorado until 1867. Of course there are differences, and the most noticeable is that Golden sits at the base of the foothills of the Rocky Mountains and is surrounded by flattop mesas with Clear Creek running through the town. Since the downtown's revitalization in the 1990s, the town has become a real draw for locals and tourists wanting a mountainesque day trip without the drive into the mountains.

Walk Description

This walk starts on the Colorado School of Mines campus in front of the historic ❶ **Guggenheim Building,** which opened in 1906 and was the home of the first geologic museum on the campus. The building is named for Simon Guggenheim, a one-time US Senator from Colorado.

It makes sense that as the West was being explored and mined for its precious metals, people would need to study metallurgy. The school began as a liberal arts and theology college in 1869, then with support from the state legislature added a School of Mines in 1873, and by 1874 became the Territorial School of Mines minus the original liberal arts and theology campus. The Colorado School of Mines has been a state institution since 1876, when Colorado became a state. Today the school's focus has expanded to environment and energy studies, as well as engineering.

The enormous white *M* on the side of the hill west of Golden was first "built" in 1908 and electrified in 1932 so it is visible day or night.

Walk north on Illinois Street through the campus. As you cross 13th Street, note that the ❷ **School of Mines Geology Museum** is to the left on the corner of Maple Street. It's free to go in and see fossils, meteorites, gemstones, moon rocks, and to learn about the state's mining history.

Look to the right down 13th Street and you should also be able to see the Armory Building, which might just be the country's largest cobblestone building. It's made from Clear Creek boulders that were dragged over by the wagonload by James Gow in 1913. This served as part of the Colorado National Guard Armory and Golden's post office until 1971. It is now office and retail space.

The next two blocks are part of the Twelfth Street Historic District that includes wood-frame and brick houses built in the late 1800s and early 1900s. Many of the houses were home to faculty members on the School of Mines campus in the early 1900s.

Two blocks to the right down 12th Street is the ❸ **Astor House Museum,** a white two-story former boardinghouse that was in business, under a few different owners and names, from its opening in 1867 until 1971. Saved from demolition, it is now a museum showing off the 18-inch-thick stone walls of Golden's first stone building, and several rooms—kitchen, dining rooms, five bedrooms—have been outfitted to look like you've stepped back in time to the early 1900s. Go out on the balcony for a different view of Golden.

After crossing 11th Street you will be in ❹ **Clear Creek History Park** on the south side of Clear Creek. When housing development encroached on a historic ranch about 15 miles from Golden, preservationists stepped in and moved many of the original buildings to this site—log by log—and then reconstructed them. The buildings are from the Pearce Ranch in nearby Golden Gate Canyon and include a schoolhouse, cabins, blacksmith shop, and chicken coop, all from the 1800s. There are tours, classes, and crafts offered at the park.

Kid Tip: In the history park, you can run around, climb up a ladder secured on an old house, and walk down the path to see chickens, and all of that makes this my favorite part of this walk and really different from the other walks in this book. Oh, look in the old schoolhouse—so different than where I go to school!

Walk over the Billy Drew Footbridge, but not too fast! If you stop in the middle of the bridge and look west you might see kayakers and canoeists in the Clear Creek Whitewater Park. The man-made chutes run for a quarter mile of the creek and are used for championship races as well as practice runs.

Turn right onto the path alongside Clear Creek after crossing the footbridge. On your left between Cheyenne Street and Arapahoe Street is the ❺ **Golden History Center.** This museum has artifacts from Golden's mining and agricultural past, as well as books, photographs, and other items that tell the story of this small town and the Native Americans who were here before the town was founded.

Turn left from the creekside path and walk up the stairs just before the Washington Avenue Bridge. If you have breezed by the museums, the bridge's signs and historical photos also tell the story of Golden. There is also a good view of Castle Rock to the east from the bridge.

Turn right at the top of the stairs and walk to the Washington Avenue Bridge. Directly across Washington Avenue is Parfet Park, the town's oldest park and a lovely spot for a picnic in summer.

To the north of Parfet Park is the ❻ **American Mountaineering Center** in the old high school. The center is home to several climbing organizations and also the ❼ **Bradford Washburn American Mountaineering Museum.** The museum has exhibits about mountain and rock climbing all over the world.

The bigger-than-life bronze statue greeting you at the bridge is Buffalo Bill, who is further commemorated every summer during Buffalo Bill Days. What started in the 1950s as a trek up to the celebrated frontiersman's grave has grown into Golden's largest annual festival that includes a parade and Wild West Show with Buffalo Bill look-alikes.

Walk south over the Washington Avenue Bridge and continue on Washington Avenue.

HOWDY FOLKS! That big sign ahead has been welcoming, well, folks to Golden since 1949. According to the Golden Pioneer Museum's book about the town, the sign was changed to say "Where The West Lives" during a renovation in the 1970s because the previous tagline, "Where the Rest Remains," had negative connotations for some people.

To your right is the ❽ **Golden Hotel,** with rooms and a restaurant that overlook Clear Creek. The Bridgewater Grill serves steaks, burgers, and a mix of fine and casual dining options.

At 12th Street look to the east and you will see the iconic red-and-white Coors sign painted on the side of the brewery. According to the Golden Pioneer Museum book, Adolphus Kuhrs (more commonly known as Adolf Coors) came from Germany in 1873 and cofounded the brewery, which was an instant success. There are tours, tastings, and a gift shop at what is now ❾ **MillerCoors**.

Continue walking south on Washington Avenue. The next few blocks offer an assortment of shops, bars, and restaurants to sample.

The ❿ **Old Capitol Grill** is located in the old capitol building from that brief time when Golden City was the capital. Built in the 1860s, it housed the first legislature session, and over the years it was also a mercantile building and a saloon featuring Coors beer.

The name sums up what you'll find at ⓫ **Golden Sweets Ice Cream & Chocolate,** a summertime favorite for locals and visitors.

⓬ **Table Mountain Inn** started out as the Spanish-style Hotel Berrimoor in 1925, and after a couple of other reincarnations it was redeveloped and reopened in 1998 to be the Southwestern-style hotel it is today. Their grill and cantina have catbird seats on the patio overlooking the goings-on along Washington Avenue.

At the corner of Washington Avenue and 15th Street is the ⓭ **Foothills Art Center** in a church built in 1872. A Victorian-era house provides additional art display space next door, and a sculpture garden outside also has changing exhibits.

On the other side of the Foothills Art Center is the ⓮ **Sherpa House Restaurant and Cultural Center**—a logical fit with the mountain clubs just down the street—serving traditional Nepalese food.

Turn right and walk west up 15th Street back to the School of Mines campus to end the walk.

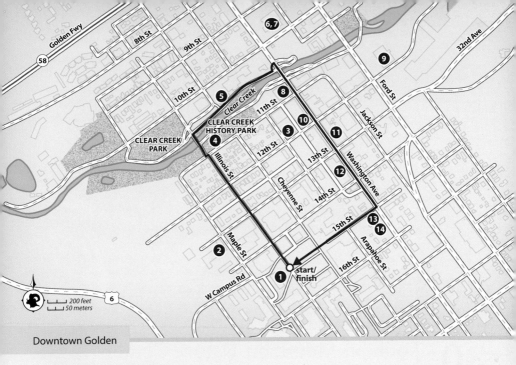

Downtown Golden

Points of Interest

1. **Guggenheim Building** 1500 Illinois St., 303-273-3000, mines.edu

2. **Geology Museum** 1301 Maple St., 303-273-3823, mines.edu/Geology_Museum

3. **Astor House Museum** 822 12th St., 303-278-3557, goldenhistory.org

4. **Clear Creek History Park** 11th St. between Illinois and Arapahoe Sts., 303-278-3557, goldenhistory.org

5. **Golden History Center** 923 10th St., 303-278-3557, goldenhistory.org

6. **American Mountaineering Center** 710 10th St., 303-996-2755

7. **Bradford Washburn American Mountaineering Museum** 710 10th St., 303-996-2755

8. **The Golden Hotel** 800 11th St., 303-279-0100, thegoldenhotel.com

9. **MillerCoors** 1221 Ford St., 800-642-6116, millercoors.com

10. **Old Capitol Grill & Smokehouse** 1122 Washington Ave., 303-279-6390

11. **Golden Sweets Ice Cream & Chocolate** 1299 Washington Ave., 303-271-1191, golden-sweets.com

12. **Table Mountain Inn** 1310 Washington St., 303-216-8040, tablemountaininn.com

13. **Foothills Art Center** 809 15th St., 303-279-3922, foothillsartcenter.org

14. **Sherpa House** 1518 Washington Ave., 303-278-7939, ussherpahouse.com

30 Lookout Mountain Nature Center and Preserve: View in Reverse

Above: *Learn about the forest in which you're hiking at Lookout Mountain Nature Center and Preserve.*

BOUNDARIES: Lookout Mountain Nature Preserve
DISTANCE: 1.4 miles
DIFFICULTY: Moderate
PARKING: Free parking is available in the parking lots at the center.
PUBLIC TRANSIT: None

What started out as a summer home in 1917 for one of Colorado's more prominent families has been turned into a nature retreat for everyone to enjoy. Only about a 20-minute drive from downtown Denver, Lookout Mountain Nature Center and Preserve is a 134-acre corner of forest-land that overlooks Denver and the eastern plains. After so many walks with views of the distant mountains *from* Denver, now you get to turn around and look down at what was once called the Queen City of the Plains. From up here, that moniker makes more sense than the Mile High

City. This is a perfect walk for families with young children, as it gives little ones a taste of the mountains and the thrill of seeing some wildlife with the comfort of picnic tables and benches, plus educational materials and displays inside and outside.

Walk Description

Begin the walk at the entrance of the ❶ **Lookout Mountain Nature Center.** While the preserve is open daily from 8 a.m. to dusk, the center itself is closed on Mondays and has seasonal hours on weekdays and weekends. It's a bonus to be able to go inside and learn about the wildlife, fauna, and history of the area. Displays include preserved animals and interactive components such as wildlife sounds. There are also maps and brochures for nearby trails, as well as staff members to answer any questions. Lookout Mountain Nature Center has many guided programs and walks throughout the year for children and their adults. Be aware that the elevation here is over 7,500 feet above sea level, and any increase in elevation means a decrease in oxygen. Always drink extra water and rest frequently. And remember to stay on the marked trail at all times during the walk.

Walk south from the nature center through the picnic tables. The ❷ **Boettcher Mansion** will be straight ahead.

Charles Boettcher came to the United States from Germany as a teenager and got rich by opening hardware stores starting in Cheyenne, Wyoming, then moving to a handful of Colorado towns. After building a mansion in Denver (since demolished), entrepreneur Boettcher reinvented himself rather than retire. He then invested in agriculture and cement and became a co-owner of the Brown Palace Hotel (see Walk 6).

This summerhouse for the Boettcher family was built in 1917 in the Arts and Crafts style and blends harmoniously with the natural setting as rocks make up the fireplace and other walls and also provide the structure for a gazebo in the garden. The house was used as a hunting lodge and for grand parties during Charles Boettcher's lifetime. Then it was a private home for Boettcher

Boettcher Mansion design details

family members until they donated it for use as a park and open space in 1972. It housed the nature center until 1997, when the new building opened. Today, when it is not being used for weddings and other private events, it is open to the public and includes a gift shop with many Arts and Crafts–style items. There is a three-panel sign northeast of the carriage house that gives a more detailed history of the house and the Boettcher family.

Turn left so that the closed gazebo is on your left as you begin walking east on the trail. Although you are always in sight of civilization (the preserve is fenced, and roads loop around the perimeter) on this walk, you are undoubtedly in the mountains and it is a very different feel than taking a walk in a city park with evergreen trees and native plants. The wind rustles through the high treetops of the ponderosa pines, and the air is a tad bit cooler up here than in Denver.

Turn right when you come to a sign marked FOREST LOOP at a fork in the trail. You are on Meadow Loop Trail, but those signs appear later. As you put some distance between yourself and the nature center and mansion, you might hear birds chirping and even see them flitting between the trees.

Kid Tip: Along the walk, you will see (treasure) boxes. See if they're open, or not. If they are, you might put a "treasure" (a cool rock or stick you found on the walk) in there, maybe for somebody else to find. Or maybe you'll find a special item someone else left for you to find. I liked the surprise of finding each box as we walked.

You will also see one of the handful of signs that dot the trail with information about the trees, insects, and fire conditions of this forest.

When you come to a small grove of scraggly aspen trees, stop to look at the blackened bark. This is a sign of the elk that also visit the preserve and rub their antlers on these trees during their rutting season. Deer are more frequent visitors, or more like coresidents, to these foothills, and there is a good chance of seeing them here.

The best time to see any wildlife at the preserve is in the morning, but you are likely to hear the pips, squeaks, and twitters of little animals and birds during this walk at any time of day. Or if it's a busy day, you will probably hear the squeal of excited children saying things like, "Look at that bird!" or "It's a deer!" to their family and friends.

Just beyond the aspen trees, the view of the eastern plains below opens up and can be quite spectacular on clear days.

As the trail turns west again, the birds become more evident in the open meadows.

Continue walking straight when you come to a sign marked MEADOW LOOP about halfway along the trail. The trail gets a little steep when you are in sight of the mansion ahead.

Turn right just past the closed gazebo and walk back to the nature center.

Backstory: Not Just Wilderness, the Wild West

You just can't get back to nature without some souvenirs to take home. About a two-minute drive or a half-mile walk from the Lookout Mountain Nature Center and Preserve is a tourist hotspot —the Buffalo Bill Museum and Grave (987½ Lookout Mountain Rd., 303-526-0747, buffalobill.org). At the same time Charles Boettcher was building the Lorraine Lodge in 1917, cattle herder, gold miner, Pony Express rider, army scout, buffalo hunter, and, most importantly, showman William F. Cody was being buried on Lookout Mountain.

Join the crowds and take a look at the white stone grave (free), go through the museum (not free), have a bite to eat at the Pahaska Teepee café and gift shop—buffalo burgers on the menu, of course—and take in the views to both the east and west from this aptly named mountaintop.

Sophie checks out Buffalo Bill's grave.

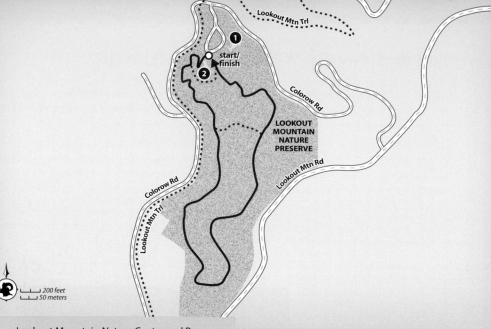

Lookout Mountain Nature Center and Preserve

Points of Interest

1 **Lookout Mountain Nature Center** 910 Colorow Rd., Golden; 720-497-7600;
jeffco.us/open-space/parks/lookout-mountain-nature-center

2 **Boettcher Mansion** 900 Colorow Rd., Golden; 720-497-7630; jeffco.us/boettcher-mansion

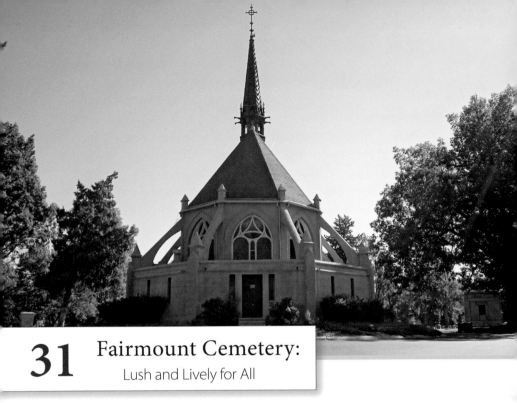

Above: Fairmount Cemetery's Little Ivy Chapel is one of two Denver Historic Landmark buildings on the cemetery grounds.

BOUNDARIES: Alameda Ave., Quebec St.
DISTANCE: Approx. 2 miles
DIFFICULTY: Easy
PARKING: Free parking is available in Fairmount's own lot, but keep in mind that gates automatically lock at sundown.
PUBLIC TRANSIT: The RTD 3 or 3L will take you to stops near Fairmount.

Fairmount Cemetery is Denver's second-oldest cemetery, founded in 1890, and the final resting place for many of Denver's most prominent names—founders, pioneers, businessmen and women, philanthropists, and more. Fairmount is like a country club for the deceased, with its manicured lawns, incredible statuary, abundant wildlife, rose garden, and an event calendar inviting the public to spend time on the grounds. It's common to see people walking their dogs past historic mausoleums and under the generous shade of an oak tree or zipping past on their bicycles on a nature trail that shares the property. The same company owns Riverside Cemetery, which, as noted in Walk 12, is a barely tended, dried-out no-man's-land in an industrial corner of the city. Both cemeteries have a list of Colorado's who's who buried there and historic one-of-a-kind statuary. At one time, both cemeteries were on service lines for trolley cars. However, Riverside's location became problematic early on when railroad tracks were laid alongside the perimeter, slaughterhouses were erected and eventually oil refineries, and it became more and more isolated. In contrast, homes primarily grew up around Fairmount and it evolved as a sort of public park—an emerald jewel of respectful solitude. It is recommended that you pair these walks of Denver's most historic burial places.

Note: The 20 miles of roads within Fairmount Cemetery are used by cars and maintenance vehicles, so always stay on the shoulder of the roads for your own safety. Fairmount Cemetery is open daily from sunrise to sunset.

Walk Description

Begin the walk in front of the ❶ **Little Ivy Chapel.** This is one of two Denver Historic Landmark buildings on the property. According to Fairmount's own research, the chapel was built in 1890 in the "style of 13th century Ecclesiastical French Gothic, and features gargoyles and flying buttresses."

❷ **Fairmount Cemetery** is private property, and all archival information about the cemetery is copyrighted by them and most is not reprintable here. However, they do sell brochures in their main office building for self-guided tours with different themes and also offer guided tours throughout the year. Tours include Trail of Trees to show off the state's largest arboretum (including an English Oak planted in 1890, the same year Fairmount was founded), June and July tours of roses in bloom, art and sculpture, architects of Denver, and more who's who of Colorado. In addition, Fairmount hosts many events to encourage visitation by the public.

Facing the chapel and looking to your right you will see the 33-foot-tall marker for the Iliff family. According to Annette L. Student's book *Denver's Riverside Cemetery: Where History Lies,* Elizabeth Iliff had not only this 65-ton monument moved from Riverside Cemetery to Fairmount Cemetery in 1920 but also the bodies buried beneath it. Her husband, John W. Iliff, was known as the first "Cattle King" for his huge and successful cattle ranches in Colorado and Wyoming starting in the 1860s and 1870s. Family donations made possible the Iliff School of Theology at the University of Denver (see Walk 23), and Iliff Avenue here in Denver is named after the family.

The statue on top is of the goddess Minerva and was installed in the center circle of section 7 at Riverside in 1880 before its relocation.

Facing south begin walking down the road into the 300-acre cemetery.

Turn left to walk east between section 3 (on your left) and section A (on your right with the large obelisk that reads LIFE). This road takes you through the middle of the historic part of the cemetery and is sometimes called "Millionaire's Row" for the many wealthy people laid to rest here.

To your left in section 4 is the headstone for William N. Byers and family, marked simply with the word PIONEER on it below his name. Byers was the founder of the *Rocky Mountain News* in 1859. His former home can be seen on Walk 2, and a branch library named after him is seen on Walk 3.

The canopy of trees provides not only dappled shade on this walk but also a home for many chirping and whistling birds that live in the cemetery. In spring flowers bloom, and lush freshly mown lawns surround all of the mausoleums, headstones, statues, and other markers throughout the grounds. In winter a fresh layer of white snow makes this peaceful place even more quiet and contemplative.

At the path opening there is a roundabout, section 91, which has the Bonfils-Stanton mausoleum monument. May Bonfils-Stanton was the daughter of *Denver Post* owner Frederick Bonfils and a philanthropist, whose contributions are remembered throughout the city to this day.

The immense and stunning ❸ Fairmount Mausoleum just ahead with large Greek columns out front and marble walls and floors inside was built in 1929 (yes, during the Depression) and opened in 1930. According to Fairmount records, "The Fairmount Mausoleum contains the sacred remains of more than 15,000 people." Notable names include Helen Bonfils—sister of the above-mentioned May Bonfils-Stanton and also a generous philanthropist to Denver institutions; Charles Boettcher, a German immigrant who made a fortune in everything from mercantile to agriculture to cement, and his fortune has gone on to fund many familiar Denver cultural places such as the Boettcher Conservatory at the Denver Botanic Gardens (see Walk 18), Boettcher Concert Hall at the Denver Center for the Performing Arts (see Walk 6), and the Boettcher Mansion (see Walk 30); and Dr. Florence Sabin, a pioneering scientist whose work significantly aided tuberculosis treatments.

As you walk right with section 89 on your right, you will see the ❹ Temple Hoyne Buell Monument on your left with its glittering gold statues and details. Buell was an architect who is best remembered for the Paramount Theatre (see Walk 6) and the first Cherry Creek Mall, which became a prototype for future malls. The Temple Hoyne Buell Theatre in the Denver Performing Arts Complex is also on Walk 6.

Turn right when the road comes to a T. You are now walking parallel to the ❺ Highline Canal; the reason Fairmount was established here was for access to this historic waterway to irrigate the non-native trees and plants throughout the cemetery. Bicyclers, dog walkers, and other recreationists use the path as it cuts through this corner of the cemetery, and this is the place in the cemetery you are most likely to see wildlife such as deer and foxes. You can visit other parts of the trail in the Highline Canal, where pedestrians and cyclists can enjoy a nature stroll or ride on the southern edge of the metro area. The canal is dry at times, particularly autumn and winter. Now that you are facing west, you get a peek of the Rocky Mountains just over the treetops.

Follow the right fork of the path to walk with section 86 on your right.

Turn right to walk with section 85 on your left and section 86 on your right. To your left is the cemetery's rose garden, which peaks in summer and includes many heirloom varieties. There is an annual heritage rose tour here, and the roses are featured on other cemetery walks.

On your right near the north end of section 86 you will see a gray obelisk for Evans family members, including Anne Evans, daughter of Colorado's former territorial governor, John Evans, who is buried at Riverside Cemetery. Anne Evans was instrumental in creating early collections—particularly Western art and Native American art—at the Denver Art Museum (see Walk 2) and cofounded the Central City Opera Association.

Continue walking north on this road to section 39, which is in the military cemetery areas. According to Fairmount's own research, "the state of Colorado purchased land at Fairmount in 1900 for deceased Spanish-American War soldiers," and the areas have grown to include hundreds of veterans.

Turn left to walk west with section 11 on your left and section 12 on your right.

The walk ends when you reach the Little Ivy Chapel again.

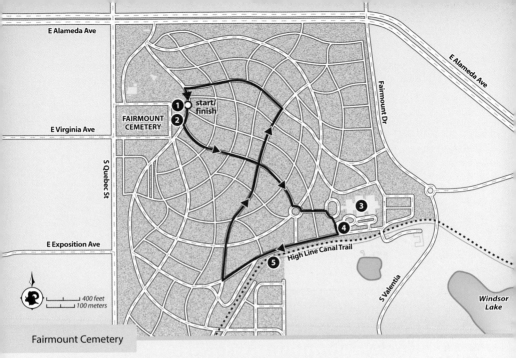

E Alameda Ave

E Alameda Ave

E Virginia Ave

FAIRMOUNT
CEMETERY

start/
finish

S Quebec St

Fairmount Dr

E Exposition Ave

High Line Canal Trail

S Valentia

Windsor
Lake

400 feet
100 meters

Fairmount Cemetery

Points of Interest

1 Little Ivy Chapel

2 Fairmount Cemetery 430 S. Quebec St., 303-399-0692, fairmount-cemetery.com

3 Fairmount Mausoleum

4 Temple Hoyne Buell Monument

5 Highline Canal

32 Rocky Mountain Arsenal National Wildlife Refuge: Where the Plains Begin

Above: Walk along the floating bridge at Rocky Mountain Arsenal National Wildlife Refuge.

BOUNDARIES: 56th Ave., Pena Blvd., 96th Ave., Quebec Pkwy. in Commerce City
DISTANCE: 1.5 miles
DIFFICULTY: Easy
PARKING: Free parking lots
PUBLIC TRANSIT: None

It's only when you head east of the city that you get a sense of Denver's other side: the plains. Not only can you picture the time when Native Americans lived here, following herds of buffalo, but today you also can actually see the buffalo. A large herd of these majestic animals was reintroduced to this short-grass prairie in 2007, where they joined deer, prairie dogs, coyotes, and other critters.

When Native Americans left as white settlers moved in, the land here was used for farming and raising livestock. Then, in 1942, the government "acquired" the land, close to 20,000 acres, to manufacture chemical weapons. Next, it was leased out for making agricultural chemicals. Basically, this area became toxic and was labeled a hazardous waste site. While all the poison kept the humans away, their absence was inviting to animals such as bald eagles and deer. It was during a massive cleanup that wildlife was discovered. Now a different branch of the government—the U.S. Department of Fish & Wildlife—saw the potential with more than 300 species congregating here.

Today the refuge is 15,000 acres of fishing lakes, trails, wildlife viewing, picnic tables, and wide open space within view of downtown's skyline. The visitor center tells the whole story with relics from World War II (your kids might ask what a dial-up phone is!) and wildlife displays (plus a gift shop). While the history here is disturbing, this is a sanctuary for many creatures and can be an enjoyable place to walk and learn about this land.

Note: Bring water, sunscreen, and a hat, as you are walking in exposed areas. There are restrooms at different points on the trail. The visitor center is open Wednesday–Sunday, 9 a.m.–4 p.m., but the refuge is open daily, sunrise–sunset. Occasionally the entire refuge is closed for mitigation or a federal holiday, so be sure to check that it is open before going. You can only see the bison from a distance or during the wildlife drive, as it is not safe to walk near them. No running or jogging is permitted on trails.

Walk Description

There are 10 miles of hiking trails here, but this walk combines portions of three of them for an easy 1.5-mile trek, though I think you can link more if you have the time and stamina. The best time to come here is sunrise or sunset to see wildlife. Signs clearly mark which areas are designated for visitors.

Follow the road signs to the trails once inside the boundaries of the Rocky Mountain Arsenal National Wildlife Refuge. Take a right turn off Havana Street to the Contact Station and park in the lot for the Lake Mary Loop Trail. The trail begins just to the left of a large sign with maps and other useful information. You will be walking south toward little Lake Mary. Go left when the trail forks and briefly walk east. You'll be passing by signs that identify the different types of prairie grasses.

Go right at the next fork. Almost straight ahead is a fishing dock, but don't stop there. Turn left at the large brown sign, and keep walking toward the floating bridge.

Kid Tip: This bridge moves while you walk on it! It's like walking on the water, not just over the water like other bridges.

For some reason, I always see more people fishing from this bridge than the fishing docks. As you continue into these wetlands, you'll hear the trilling of red-winged blackbirds and other songbirds—and maybe even see a fish jump out of the water! One time we saw a snake "swim" (slither?) across the water here.

After you pop out of the cattails and other tall wetland plant life, go right on the trail. You'll hear lots of birdcalls and maybe even see them perched on one of the birdhouses.

Soon you'll see a sign for the Prairie Trail. The loop around Lake Mary is just a little over half a mile, so I encourage you not to finish the loop yet. Go left when you see the sign for the Prairie Trail. This dips down into what can be quite marshy depending on the season and recent weather—we've heard and seen frogs here.

The trail soon zigzags uphill and—ta-da!—there is a view of the Rocky Mountains to the west and downtown Denver's skyline. While the plains don't have the dramatic scenery of the mountains, there is a real beauty and diversity here. This portion of the trail goes through a prairie dog town, and you're likely to hear them chattering, calling out a warning to one another about your presence. I've seen rabbits and deer on this trail too. Take a minute to sit on the bench placed along the trail and soak up the view to the east before going on.

The trail suddenly crosses an old road (Joliet Street, to be exact). Go left toward the barrier, then right into a parking lot where there is a restroom. Resume the trail to the right of the map sign. You'll now be walking northeast toward Lake Ladora. As the trail winds along, you'll notice that this stunning prairie includes many varieties of wildflowers, and you might also see more birds, or just hear them.

Turn left just before you reach the bench under the large cottonwood tree. You are now heading west again with the lake on your right. This is part of the Lake Ladora Loop Trail.

Shortly, possibly with the sounds of meadowlarks singing nearby, you'll reach the road again. Turn right and walk until you see a sign on your left that reads, "Lake Mary Loop Trail" with an arrow pointing to the right. Go left on the trail here and then follow it as it veers right until you reach a small bridge (a wooden staircase is to your right) and go left. You have arrived back at the floating walkway! I recommend finishing the loop around Lake Mary by going straight ahead, but that floating walkway might tempt you again. Either way, you'll soon be within sight of the parking lot again.

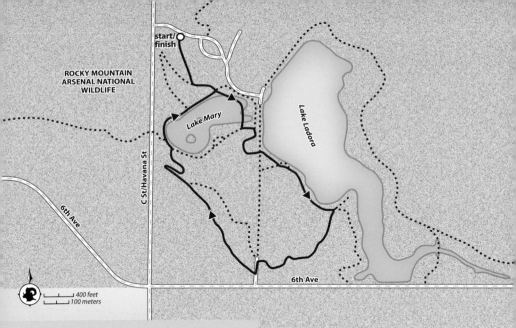

Rocky Mountain Arsenal National Wildlife Refuge

Point of Interest

1 **Rocky Mountain Arsenal National Wildlife Refuge Visitor Center** 6550 Gateway Rd., Commerce City; 303-289-0232; fws.gov/refuge/Rocky_Mountain_Arsenal

Appendix: Walks by Theme

Architecture

Art and Culture

History

Time to Eat

Water

Index

About the Authors

Curt Hjelle

Mindy Sink wrote the first edition of *Walking Denver* and is also the author of Moon Handbooks *Guide to Denver* and a coauthor of *Colorado Organic: Cooking Seasonally, Eating Locally.* She has written extensively for *The New York Times,* and her work has also appeared in *The Christian Science Monitor, Sunset Magazine,* and many other well-known publications and websites.

Mindy lives in Denver with her husband and their daughter —whose school is, of course, within walking distance from their home.

To learn more about Mindy, go to mindysink.com.

Sophie Seymour is in middle school and lives in the Highlands neighborhood (see Walks 8, 9, 10, and 11). In addition to urban walks, she enjoys running, skiing, writing, reading, and studying epidemiology.